GETTING YOUR HUSBAND
to TALK *to* YOU

GETTING YOUR HUSBAND
to TALK to YOU

Bob and Cheryl
MOELLER

HARVEST HOUSE PUBLISHERS
EUGENE, OREGON

Cover design by Koechel Peterson & Associates, Inc., Minneapolis, Minnesota

Cover photo © Brand X Pictures / Thinkstock

The authors are represented by MacGregor Literary, Inc. of Hillsboro, Oregon.

This book contains stories in which the authors have changed people's names and some details of their situations in order to protect their privacy.

GETTING YOUR HUSBAND TO TALK TO YOU
Copyright © 2013 by Bob and Cheryl Moeller
Published by Harvest House Publishers
Eugene, Oregon 97402
www.harvesthousepublishers.com

Library of Congress Cataloging-in-Publication Data
  Moeller, Bob.
    Getting your husband to talk to you / Bob and Cheryl Moeller.
    pages cm
  ISBN 978-0-7369-5201-9 (pbk.)
  ISBN 978-0-7369-5202-6 (eBook)

1. Marriage—Religious aspects—Christianity. 2. Communication in marriage. 3. Men—Psychology. 4. Interpersonal communication—Religious aspects—Christianity. 5. Man-woman relationships—Religious aspects—Christianity. I. Title.
BV835.M6425 2013
248.8'44--dc23
                                                                    2012048918

Printed in the United States of America

13 14 15 16 17 18 19 20 21 22 / BP-CD / 10 9 8 7 6 5 4 3 2 1

To Pastor Rob and Christine Nelson
and Pastor Andrew and Tiffany Moeller
and the wonderful people of Bethany Church in Chicago.
You opened your church and your hearts to us as a home for our ministry.
We thank God for you and will be forever grateful for your love and kindness.

Contents

A Word from the Authors

Many husbands talk freely and openly from their hearts with their wives. If that's the case in your marriage, you probably don't need this book.

However, if you wish that your husband would talk to you—or talk to you more often—or talk to you on a deeper level—then we believe this book will help you. What we offer are principles and techniques that we have seen work time and again in getting husbands who typically don't talk—or don't talk much—to begin sharing their thoughts, feelings, and emotions with their wife. When that happens, she hears things locked away in his heart for years or even decades. He feels drawn to her, and she feels drawn to him, and the result is game-changing.

The stories, examples, and illustrations used in this book are taken from actual situations, but the details and settings have been changed to protect identities. In some cases we create a composite picture of one or more marriages to illustrate a particular truth or idea. We also realize that for every principle we share there may be an exception. Maybe in your marriage your husband talks but you don't. If that's the case, there still is help, insight, and benefit to be gained from reading this book. You simply have your husband apply many of the techniques and principles toward you rather than you applying them toward him.

As you begin this journey of getting your husband to talk to you, may you experience afresh the wisdom, power, and truth of God's Word to transform your marriage.

"My dear brothers and sisters, take note of this. Everyone should be quick to listen, slow to speak and slow to become angry" (James 1:19).

Bob and Cheryl Moeller

Introduction

Do Men Lack the Ability to Talk?

Bob was in his midthirties and living out West when a couple having trouble with their marriage approached him for help. It was apparent the wife was seriously considering a divorce. The issue wasn't marital infidelity or domestic abuse or a pornography addiction.

"Dan won't talk," Joan simply said. "Go ahead and see if you can get him to talk. It won't do any good."

Bob wasn't quite sure what to do. Joan sounded so certain and so convincing that perhaps she was right—perhaps Dan simply couldn't talk to people.

But Bob decided to take her up on her dare to see if he could get Dan to talk. He nervously invited Dan to have lunch at a local hamburger place and was surprised when Dan readily agreed.

For the next few days Bob rehearsed in his mind the different questions he might ask Dan to get him to talk. He compiled a mental list of things to keep the conversation from turning into "dead air," as they say in radio.

The day arrived when Bob and Dan sat down to lunch. After exchanging a few cordialities, glancing over the menu, and placing a double order of burgers, fries, and soft drinks, Bob hesitated a moment, cleared his throat, and jumped off the end of the conversational diving board.

"So, Dan, how are you?" he asked (an anemic question if there ever was one).

What happened next stunned Bob and would eventually serve to change the course of our ministry to struggling couples.

Dan began to talk.

Not only did he begin to talk, he talked on and on. Thirty minutes into Dan's soliloquy, Bob realized he had said less than a dozen words. Forty-five minutes into the monologue, Dan was just hitting his stride as he discussed his car, his cat, and his time spent in college. As the hour neared conclusion, Bob concluded he was never going to get a word in edgewise.

Doesn't Dan want to know anything about me?

As the clock struck one, Dan was all smiles. He stood up and shook Bob's hand and thanked him for the lunch. As Dan left and walked happily to his car, Bob was left sitting there in confusion (as well as with the check for lunch).

What just happened here? Bob thought as he stared toward the parking lot. *His wife told me that Dan didn't have the ability to talk.* Dan had not only talked, he had talked and talked and talked to the point of being rude.

As Bob drove back to the office, a glimmer of truth about men and conversation began to flicker on. *Maybe there aren't any men who can't talk*, Bob mused. *Maybe there are only some men who have never been listened to.*

1

The Most Common Reasons Men Don't Talk to Their Wives

"My dear brothers and sisters, take note of this: Everyone should be quick to listen, slow to speak and slow to become angry."

JAMES 1:19

Through the years we have noticed an interesting pattern with wives who complain about their husband's inability to talk. Usually the wives are more outgoing and talkative while their husbands tend to be more quiet and withdrawn. The conclusion is typically this: the wife was born with the gift of talking while the husband was not.

However, we beg to differ. Simply because the husband does not feel comfortable talking to his wife does not mean he lacks the gifts to do so. As the story in the introduction illustrates, Dan, who was typically silent and unengaged, demonstrated his ability to become extremely talkative given the right setting.

Perhaps talking is not a matter of gifting but of opportunity.

Stalemate or Stale Mate?

Several years ago we sat with a couple having marital problems and listened to their story. They had enjoyed getting to know each other during the courtship and engagement period, but now the husband had almost entirely quit talking. Even as they discussed their marriage issues with us, he would frequently turn to her and say, "Would you agree? Am I right?" It was as if he needed her validation or approval before he could go on.

She, on the other hand, was very skilled and certain in describing her hurt feelings, disappointed expectations, and deep feelings of rejection—particularly in the communication aspect of their marriage.

That couple fits a pattern we often see: the husband has shut down verbally and the wife is slowly dying inside for lack of conversation. The man is reluctant to venture his thoughts and feelings while the woman is more than willing to share hers. They have reached a stalemate in their marriage. She is ready to give up, and he is ready to consider other options (worst-case scenario, a girlfriend at the office or a new love interest on the Internet).

What's going on here? Why isn't the husband talking? Why is the wife in such deep pain? Did they each simply marry the wrong person?

We believe there are reasons why men won't talk in a marriage or a relationship. And no, we don't believe they married the wrong person and should consider a divorce, find a new lover, or live out their remaining days in misery and sullenness.

Why Men Don't Talk

To begin addressing and resolving this seemingly impossible impasse, we must understand why men don't talk. We offer here what we believe are seven of the most common reasons.

---

1. Men don't talk because they are afraid their thoughts and ideas will be criticized and rejected.

The Bible recognizes that men are motivated by respect and honor. Perhaps the most succinct statement of this principle is found in Ephesians 5:33: "However, each one of you also must love his wife as he loves himself, *and the wife must respect her husband.*"

It doesn't say that the wife is to agree with her husband on everything he thinks. Nor does it say she is to say yes when she means no or to practice blind obedience. The Scriptures say she is to "respect her husband." What does that mean, particularly when it comes to getting him to talk? It means, in biblical terms, she "should be quick to listen, slow to speak and slow to become angry" (James 1:19).

A wife should listen with an accepting, nonjudgmental, and honoring attitude even if she doesn't agree with everything her husband says or thinks.

The Miracle of Hearing His Story

One of the methods we use to help couples get to the root problems in their marriage is to ask each of them to share their life's story with us. We will take out a spiral-bound notebook and ask the person to begin by telling us their earliest recollections of the home they grew up in. What do they remember first about their lives? How did their parents get along? What was the atmosphere of their home?

"I'm not going to say much," Bob typically says to the husband. "I'm just going to listen, and if you don't mind, I'm going to write down your thoughts so I have a record of this."

"Good luck getting him to talk," the wife will sometimes say. "He hasn't said ten words to me this week."

"That's all right," Bob says. "I'm in no hurry. Let's just start with your earliest days. What do you remember?"

There is often a brief period of silence, but that's okay. To get a man to talk you must welcome periods of silence, not fear them. After ten seconds or so, the man will usually clear his throat and say, "Well, I guess the earliest I remember was about three years of age. My dad was a machinist. We lived near my grandparents…"

As the man begins to share his life story, he often looks at us with some tentativeness, reading our faces for some kind of response. We simply smile and nod and encourage him to go on. And usually he does—sometimes for hours. It is not at all untypical for Bob to get four to six pages of single-spaced notes from the husband in a two- to three-hour period. As the man relaxes and opens up about his life, his wife will often look over at him with an expression nothing short of amazement.

"Oh, I'm sorry," the man will often say. "I've taken up all our time today. I didn't mean to do that."

"That's okay," we respond. "We have all the time in the world. We truly appreciate you sharing your life story with us."

Avoid the Rejection Notice

What just happened? The husband, who is supposedly unwilling if not incapable of talking, has just spent the last two to three hours talking nearly nonstop. During that time he has occasionally stopped to brush back tears and, in some cases, been unable to carry on until he regained control of his emotions. We've seen that happen with mechanics, doctors, police officers, lawyers, construction workers, and a whole host of "man's man" husbands.

Meanwhile their wife is sitting next to them thinking, *Why won't he do that for me?*

That's an excellent question and deserves an honest answer: *Men will not talk if they think their ideas will be criticized and ultimately rejected.*

If a wife has a slightly (or significantly) stronger personality, her tendency will be to listen to her husband's thoughts or ideas until he says something that triggers a response in her. When that happens, her natural instinct is to jump in and say, "I'm sorry, but you are wrong about our daughter; her problem is not too little free time but rebellion, pure and simple," or "If you had been listening to me last Saturday, you would have known we had a soccer game tonight; but you were too busy watching the game," or "I don't know how you can possibly say that."

Statements like these, as sincere and heartfelt as they may be, often have the unintended effect of shutting the husband down. In his mind he's thinking, *Okay, I get it. She thinks I'm wrong or don't understand or I'm just plain stupid. I don't need to be told I'm wrong all the time. I'll just be quiet. That way I can't be criticized or called out. I'm tired of feeling disrespected.*

What the husband doesn't understand is that his wife often challenges his statements, expresses disagreement, or even argues *in order to connect and find agreement.* (At least that's the conclusion of Emerson Eggerichs, author of *Love and Respect.*) But to a man it sounds like she's just picking a fight. Rather than fight, he'll verbally flatline, stonewall the conversation, or walk into another room, leaving behind one frustrated and often heartbroken wife.

Connection or Collision?

Reading Eggerichs is where we first gained the insight that *women will confront in order to connect*. While women will challenge in order to stimulate a conversation they desperately long to have, men will back away from such a challenge they desperately want to avoid. Rather than risk having their thoughts, ideas, and convictions evaluated and turned back on them in a negative light, men will simply quit talking and find an excuse to get out of there. That can trigger an instinct in the wife to turn up the verbal heat, follow her husband, and take her voice up a notch or two to try and get him to turn around and engage.

If it didn't cause so much heartache, this cycle would be almost humorous. It has much the same intended effect as someone who speaks only French talking with someone who speaks only Chinese. Despite your best intention, it won't do you any good to speak more slowly or raise your voice. The person still isn't speaking your language and hasn't a clue what you're saying, only wondering why you are acting so strange.

In short, a common mistake wives make in trying to get their husbands to talk is to evaluate or judge their ideas as soon as they are spoken. That serves only to shut husbands up. As we will say later in the book, adopting a nonjudgmental, respectful, and patient response to their words will yield far more conversation than offering an instant analysis of their thoughts or ideas.

---

2. Men don't talk because they do not believe they are as verbally skilled as their wives.

There is little question that men, on average, are physically stronger than women. We find this idea affirmed in 1 Peter 3:7: "Husbands, in the same way be considerate as you live with your wives, and treat them with respect as the weaker partner." At the same time, Peter admonishes husbands not to use their physical advantage to treat their wives in an inconsiderate or disrespectful manner. This can range all the way from mild intimidation to actual physical abuse. The misuse of the masculine physical-strength advantage is one reason the vast majority of restraining orders for domestic violence are filed against men rather than women.

Yet, God in his wisdom has brought balance to this equation by endowing women with a verbal or relational advantage over men. Again, in 1 Peter 3:1 we read, "Wives, in the same way submit yourselves to your own husbands so that, if any of them do not believe the word, they may be won over without words by the behavior of their wives."

A Bogey in Conversation

Because women are often so skilled in the use of words, men can easily feel intimated. For many husbands, engaging in an exchange of ideas with their wives is the equivalent of stepping onto a golf course to go eighteen holes against the winner of last year's Masters Tournament. Many husbands, sensing the outcome even before the first swing, will simply find an excuse to walk off the course and put their clubs back in the trunk of their car.

Actual physiological evidence exists for women often possessing superior verbal skills. The two sides of the female brain are far more connected than the two sides of the male brain, which allows women to process ideas and concepts faster and more holistically than men. Other studies have documented that women speak, on average, thirty thousand to sixty thousand words a day, while men speak fifteen to thirty thousand. Women use more words than men often because they are better equipped to do so.

The Scriptures, recognizing women's verbal advantages, unusual ability to articulate ideas, and overall attraction for words, offers some cautions. For when this giftedness is not exercised under the control of the Holy Spirit, it can result in some sad scenarios:

> Likewise, teach the older women to be reverent in the way
> they live, not to be slanderers or addicted to much wine,
> but to teach what is good (Titus 2:3).

> As for younger widows…they get into the habit of being idle and going about from house to house. And not only do they become idlers, but also busybodies who talk nonsense, saying things they ought not to (1 Timothy 5:11,13).

> In the same way, the women are to be worthy of respect, not malicious talkers but temperate and trustworthy in everything (1 Timothy 3:11).

The Bible clearly teaches that the verbal gifts women have been given can be used for good or ill. Certainly using those words for good every day is vital to the health of the marriage. But the fact that God created women with superior verbal skills should be celebrated rather than shunned. It's part of the unique, beautiful, interesting, and complementary nature of how God created males and females.

Think back to the family reunions or get-togethers you experienced as a child. Where was the noise usually coming from? For us, our mothers gathered in the kitchen with the other women of the family to prepare the meal. In Bob's case his Swedish aunts would often all talk at once, and for one to get noticed, they would have to increase their volume and talk over the others. The decibel level in the kitchen would sometimes nearly cause the dishes in the cupboards to rattle.

Where were the men as the women's conversation grew in intensity and volume? They were sitting in the living room staring at the football game on television. Occasionally questions would be asked and answered, but the atmosphere resembled more a hospital waiting room than the trading pit of the Chicago Stock Exchange in the kitchen. Was one room better than the other? No, each met the needs of the people gathered for an enjoyable afternoon with relatives. But the women found their fulfillment in conversation while the men did so in an activity like watching football without saying much.

Should You Play Ping-Pong or Catch?

What does all this have to do with getting your husband to talk? It is a common mistake to think that men are just as verbally skilled as women. While some are, most are not. For those who are not, few things are more intimidating than getting into a conversation with a wife who can use words and ideas as deftly as Michelangelo could use a paintbrush.

Perhaps the simplest way to illustrate this is to say that when women talk, they play ping-pong. When men talk, they play catch.

If you've ever watched Olympic Ping-Pong teams play for the gold, the speed is almost blinding. The competitors stand ten to fifteen feet behind the table and fire the ball back and forth at incredible speeds. A deft flick of the wrist or angle of the paddle sends the ball speeding back across the table only to be volleyed back again.

That's how women talk. Their remarkable brains process so much information so quickly and with such skill and clarity that they are able to answer before the other person has even finished their sentence. You can even add a third party to the conversation, and the verbal speed only intensifies rather than slows down. Meanwhile, men observe this verbal blizzard with an expression that goes from quizzical to dumbfounded.

Men, on the other hand, play catch when they talk to each other. They throw the ball to the other person; that person catches it and holds onto it for several seconds or even minutes before he throws it back. Men are neither frustrated nor impatient with this process. Rather, they respect each other's need to receive, and then process and respond at a pace that feels natural and comfortable.

When the wife tries to play ping-pong and the husband tries to play catch, trouble is on its way. The wife feels uncertain, confused, and frustrated by the delays in her husband's answers. When she asks a question and he responds, "I don't know what I think, give me a minute," she may think he's just being stubborn or isn't engaged. Actually, he's just running his software and trying to come up with what he really does think.

When he tosses the verbal football to her and she fires it back at him with lightning speed, he's taken off guard. Why doesn't she just hold on to it for a minute or two before throwing it back? Why is she being so aggressive with me? Is she upset? Did I say something wrong?

We all know men who are verbally skilled. They make great auctioneers, local politicians, and car salesmen. Yet, we believe they are more the exception than the rule. And in a marriage where the wife has come to the despairing conclusion that her husband won't talk, it is often the case that she possesses verbal talents and abilities he does not.

In order to get this husband to talk, it is vital that the wife learns how to play catch far more than she plays ping-pong (we will discuss in later chapters how she can do this). She will need to ask questions, and then give him generous time and space to formulate his answers. Eventually he will, and he will share those thoughts and ideas with her, just as long as he isn't staring at a ping-pong ball hurtling back toward him at the speed of light.

This attitude of respecting, honoring, and patiently listening to her husband is part of how a wife will, as the Scripture teaches, "win" her husband "without words." What exactly is meant by "winning" is something we'll explore more in later chapters.

---

3. Men don't talk because they are convinced they will lose the exchange.

The United States has traditionally produced strong Olympic men's basketball teams. One year the US team was matched against a team from a smaller country and won by almost eighty points. Regardless of whether our team deliberately ran up the score or was simply so much better they couldn't help the outcome, the other team left the game humiliated. Can you imagine how they would feel if they were invited to a rematch the next day? And the next? And the next?

When men conclude that not only are they going to lose a verbal exchange with their wives but lose it by a wide margin, they try to avoid the match altogether. While perhaps a few men will consistently compete in sports where they lose virtually every time, the majority will sooner or later decide to take up another sport. (The only exception we know of is the Chicago Cubs, who have not won a World Series in over a hundred years. Regardless, they keep showing up for spring training each year.)

I'll Take a Root Canal Instead

It's much the same with conversation in marriage. If a husband believes, despite presenting his best thoughts or ideas, he will find himself backed into a verbal corner and "lose" the exchange, he will simply find a way next time to avoid the confrontation altogether. This may include cutting the conversation short, suddenly remembering an important errand he needs to run, or just walking away and shutting the door behind him.

The husband comes to associate talking to his wife with suffering humiliation and loss of face. That's why he will do nearly anything to avoid being caught in a sit-down, face-to-face, all cards on the table conversation with his wife. He'd rather have a root canal without anesthesia than face that type of emotional pain anytime soon.

Unfortunately, the wife can read this as a lack of interest or desire to be close. She may interpret his strategic retreat from conversation as a sure sign he doesn't care or love her anymore. She will then often increase her efforts to pursue a conversation with him only to find her overtures rebuffed or ignored. This seems to only reinforce her conclusion that "he just doesn't care" or "he simply can't talk."

The Meek Shall Inherit Their Husband

What is needed if conversation is ever to be restored is an entirely new way of looking at the relationship. The husband is going to have to see his wife's efforts to start a conversation for what they are—a deep (and often desperate) desire to emotionally connect with him rather than an opportunity to spar with him verbally and score another knockout.

For the wife's part, she may have to rein in her verbal skills and use them to affirm and build up her husband rather than to quickly evaluate, challenge, or criticize his thinking or feelings. Someone once defined *meekness* as "strength under control." If that's correct, then the wife is going to have to practice a whole new level of meekness in her interactions with her husband until he feels it's safe to step onto the playing field of dialogue with her. Just as a husband must never, never use his physical strength to control or intimidate his wife, a wife must never use her verbal strength to control or intimidate her husband.

Often wives are completely unaware how their verbal agility or assertiveness can intimidate a husband. They often think they are just being honest and sharing their feelings openly with their husband, while he's feeling overwhelmed and cornered and often a bit foolish once the exchange is over. From our experience, women who intentionally use their superior verbal abilities to win battles with their husband are often coming from a place of emotional pain and insecurity (most often the result of painful childhood and adolescent experiences). They employ an aggressive verbal offense to serve as their emotional defense against rejection or hurt. Unfortunately, the husband is driven further away by her verbal aggressiveness, leaving her feeling more isolated and rejected than before.

Jim struggled with being overweight, passive-aggressive, and unhappy in his marriage. Though actually an articulate man, when matched against his wife's verbal skills and relational insights, he lost all confidence and retreated. She, in turn, became angry at him and even more critical of his performance as a husband.

We encouraged her to throttle back her verbal retorts and simply listen to Jim for long and uninterrupted periods of time, building him up and praising his strongest attributes. She took the advice, and almost immediately he began responding to her emotionally in a positive way. As she started to listen more than speak, he gained the confidence to take tentative steps onto the playing field of meaningful conversation in their marriage. He actually reached out and took her hand, something that hadn't happened in a great while.

---

4. Men don't talk because they were taught as children to shut up or face the consequences.

In college psychology classes we were introduced to the behaviorist school made famous by B.F. Skinner. Skinner believed that most human behavior could be explained by the association of rewards or punishments with certain behaviors.

For example, if a mouse in a cage pushes a lever and a piece of cheese falls down, the mouse will experience pleasure from eating the cheese and push the bar again. Each time the mouse pushes the bar and eats a piece of cheese, it reinforces pleasure in the mouse's brain. Some mice, seeking that pleasurable experience over and over again, will push the lever continuously until they are exhausted or become so satiated with cheese they can't take another bite.

However, if the researcher replaces the reward of cheese for pushing the lever with the "reward" of an electric shock, it will take only a few taps on the bar before the mouse stops touching it altogether. He quickly associates pushing the bar with jolting pain and learns that to avoid the pain, he needs to avoid touching the bar. The mouse will starve to death rather than risk experiencing another painful shock.

He May Have a Crushed Spirit

If your husband grew up in a home where whenever he tried to express his true feelings or desires he was met with harsh rebukes, demeaning comments, or even a slap across the face, it didn't take long for him to figure out it's better to shut up (and stay that way) than risk incurring his parents' wrath or punishment.

Unless those painful emotional wounds are healed, he may grow up to marry someone who continues the similar pattern of rebuke, rejection, and ridicule whenever he tries to say something. Even if his wife is far less severe in her rebuff of his thoughts or desires than his parents were, he has been conditioned to sit down, shut up, and stay out of the way.

Sadly, we hear our share of heartbreaking stories from men who were raised in verbally, emotionally, or physically abusive homes. Dylan was raised in the forties in a home where his mother and father referred to him only by the name "Wimp." They never called him Dylan. Rather, they would say, "Hey, Wimp, pass the salt," or "Wimp, go outside and get the mail." He would stand helplessly as his father and mother smiled perversely at each other each time they mocked the little boy.

Can you imagine the enormous sense of rejection, pain, and humiliation Dylan experienced growing up? Is it any wonder he struggled in his marriage to express his true feelings and desires? Is it any surprise he wrestled with explosive anger at the slightest provocation?

While an extreme example, it reveals why some men don't talk: they learned growing up that their thoughts and wishes didn't matter. Worse, if they did say something, bad things often happened. Whether it was a self-focused mother who did all the talking or a father who believed children should be seen and not heard, a husband who reaches adulthood believing it is best to shut up and keep his head low is likely to have trouble talking to his wife.

If a wife does not understand that her husband's spirit was crushed as a child and that's why he is so reluctant to open up and share his true feelings and ideas, she can mistake his silence for indifference, stubbornness, or withdrawal. If she is the more dominant of the two, she may have made the mistake of criticizing or rejecting his thoughts the few times he ventured to share them honestly. This only reinforces his perception that the less said, the better.

Stepping on Each Other's Core Pain

For things to change in their relationship, she will have to draw him out through her patience, affirmation, and acceptance. Even if she is upset with him for something he has said or done, she may have to stifle her anger or frustration. Otherwise, she risks giving him the equivalent of an electric shock and teaching him to associate pain and discomfort with talking to her.

If a wife struggles with a tendency toward dominance (control), hostility (anger), and unrealistic expectations (perfectionism), these three together will reinforce pain, inadequacy, and failure in her husband's mind and heart. She will need to get in touch with the causes of her emotional pain (again, often from the home or environment she was raised in) and seek healing for that. Both the husband and wife will have to learn how to care about what one counselor calls "each other's core pain." Rather than reacting to each other, they will have to learn to show love and compassion toward each other's wounded heart.

Imagine if a husband experienced only understanding, acceptance, and affirmation from his wife when he expressed his true thoughts, ideas, and feelings. Would he be drawn to her? We have seen over and over that when a husband is offered "a piece of cheese" rather than "an electric shock," he finds conversation with his wife almost irresistible.

One man went from calling his wife once a week when he was out of town on business to calling her twice a day. What was the difference? She quit dominating the conversation, listened respectfully to his thoughts and needs, and refrained from trying to fix him. He became almost addicted to spending time with her on the phone, something that hadn't happened since their courtship decades earlier.

---

5. Men don't talk because they are uncomfortable talking about their feelings.

Comedian Dave Barry once wrote an article titled "What Women Don't Understand about Guys" (*Reader's Digest*, January 1996). In it he chronicles the budding romance between a man named Roger and a woman named Elaine. After several weeks of seeing each other, Elaine begins to wonder if Roger is as interested in their relationship as she is. She broaches the topic one evening only to have him appear confused and uncertain. She interprets his ambivalence as a sure sign she is pushing him too soon and too hard to make a decision about the future of their relationship. Barry then offers these insightful (if not slightly unorthodox) observations on a guy's way of thinking about love and romance:

> [Roger] has a guy brain, basically an analytical, problem-solving organ. It's not comfortable with nebulous concepts such as love, need and trust. If the guy brain has to form an opinion about another person, it prefers to base it on facts, such as his or her earned-run average.
>
> Women have trouble accepting this. They are convinced that guys spend a certain amount of time thinking about the relationship. How could a guy see another human being day after day, night after night, and not be thinking about the relationship? This is what women figure.
>
> They are wrong. A guy in a relationship is like an ant standing on top of a truck tire. The ant is aware that

something large is there, but he cannot even dimly comprehend what it is. And if the truck starts to roll, the ant will sense that something important is happening, but right up until he rolls around to the bottom and is squashed, the only thought in his tiny brain will be *Huh?*

If He Doesn't Know What to Say—He Won't

Humor and overstatement aside, Dave Barry is correct that many men struggle to get in touch with their emotions and feelings. In some cases they aren't quite certain what they are feeling, while women are often finely tuned in to the exact nature of their emotions. While women can tell you they are feeling rejection, loneliness, or fear, men may be only vaguely aware of the frustration, loneliness, and hurt that's going on inside them. They just know for some reason they are hurting.

Imagine sitting down at a party with someone who has a degree in political science. While you have a passing interest in politics and elections, this person can tell you voting trends county by county within your state. While you can offer general reasons why you voted for a particular candidate in the last election, they can recite the person's voting record as a state legislator, House member, and United States senator.

How long would you continue to enjoy the conversation? How soon until you spotted someone across the room that you'd like to say hello to? Many men feel out of their depth when discussing their feelings and emotions—particularly when they are pressured or hurried to do so. Wives can often seem like professionals when it comes to defining and dissecting emotions and relationships, while men often feel like amateurs.

"Why don't you just stand up to your mother for once?" a wife demands of her husband. "You know how depressed you are when you leave her home. Isn't it time you told her how you feel?"

The reasons the husband may not stand up to his domineering mother may be many and complex, but just the thought of provoking a confrontation and the negative emotions it would produce could prove difficult for him to put into words.

When men don't know what to say, they often say nothing, and a wife may misinterpret her husband's silence as lack of interest, insensitivity, or rejection of her feelings. What in fact may be going on is the man is running the equivalent of a "full virus scan" of his emotional software to try and determine exactly how he feels about his problems.

It's not uncommon for a man to wake up the day after a distressing encounter and articulate exactly why the incident was so upsetting to him. It has taken almost twenty-four hours to process his thoughts and feelings, but now he can give them a name and likely be able to explain them with detail and conviction.

Accepting a Delayed Response

It is important that wives understand that for men, processing emotions requires time and patience before answers appear on the screen. To help their husbands sort through their various emotions and feelings, wives will need to give them generous time and space to process. This requires backing off from demanding that their husbands share right at the moment what they are feeling. Husbands may not know exactly what they are feeling—but eventually they will.

This also requires that a wife not demand an immediate resolution of a problematic situation, particularly as it may relate to relational difficulties, realizing it may take hours or even days before her husband is sure of what he wants to do.

Finally, if the husband's descriptions of his feelings lack precision, that reality should be accepted rather than criticized. Once he is ready to discuss his feelings, a wife can help him clarify his thinking, but this is often better done by asking questions rather than trying to give answers. While men may be uncomfortable talking about feelings, they still have them. A loving wife will honor those feelings and treat them with respect, even if she disagrees.

---

6. Men don't talk because they don't want to appear emotionally weak.

Clint was an active-duty noncommissioned officer who had been deployed several times. He had seen much human suffering and loss and had indications of posttraumatic stress disorder. He and his wife were having real problems in their marriage and were talking divorce.

As we listened to Clint's life story, Bob asked, "Who loved you the most growing up, and what did they do to make you feel that way?"

We've found this to be an extremely important question for a number of reasons. To begin with, it helps identify the husband's love language (Gary Chapman's term). Is it words of affirmation, gifts, physical touch, acts of service, or quality time? If a wife can discover which love language her husband naturally speaks, that can help her relate to him in a loving way that he will respond to. The same applies to a husband discovering his wife's love language. One of the real tragedies in many marriages is that both partners try to love the other person by speaking their own love language, not the other person's, and thus miss the mark.

In this case, Clint thought for a moment about who loved him the most growing up, and then a slight smile appeared on his lips. It was the first time he had smiled that day. "Aw, of course I know who it was that made me feel the most loved. It was my grandmother. My own mother had given me up when she and my dad divorced. My dad paid almost no attention to me, but my grandmother took an interest in me. She baked me cookies, helped me with my homework, and would just sit and talk with me after school."

Clint looked out the window and, emotion causing his voice to crack, said, "And when she died, I lost the only friend I had in this whole world. Why did she have to die?" At this point the tough, stoic, and seemingly detached soldier began to cry. For a minute or two the tears flowed freely, then he jerked his head up and said, "Hey, what is this junk you're doing to me?"

"You just got in touch with your heart," we responded. "No one is trying to manipulate you. You just got down to the feelings you've buried deep inside for a long time."

Underneath His Anger Is Hurt and Pain

Husbands can become uncomfortable, even angry, when they first get in touch with their feelings. It's an uncomfortable experience because in their mind it suggests they are losing control or showing weakness. They switch back to anger, which is a far more culturally acceptable means for males to process hurt (though it often does great damage to relationships). For some men, getting down to their true feelings is a new experience, and so when they do, it can seem overwhelming.

Wives, on the other hand, are usually quite comfortable displaying their emotions. One marriage author refers to women crying as their "emotional sweating." They are just getting their emotions out of their system so they can calm down inside and resolve them.

Sadly, young boys are often taught that any display of emotion is a sign of weakness. Just ask any junior high boy who dares to show tears in the presence of other male adolescents. The name-calling, shaming, and rejection they will experience can leave lifelong scars. It only takes a macho teacher calling a teenage boy who shows his emotions a "girl" in front of everyone else (it happens), and that boy will determine never to cry again.

Ironically, World War II General George S. Patton, one of the toughest leaders ever to wear a uniform, wept in front of his commanding officer when told he would be restored to his command following an incident where Patton had slapped a soldier. The lesson: real men do cry. It may not be all that often—but when they do, it's for a good reason.

The fear of appearing weak explains why a man will often go to great lengths to avoid displaying any emotion (other than anger) in the presence of his wife and children. If the topic turns to an issue that touches raw and unhealed hurts in his life, he may shut down or walk away rather than appear vulnerable. Sadly, the wife is left to feel either he doesn't care or he isn't capable of expressing his true feelings. Either way, she feels shut out of his life.

Growing Up Among the Frozen Chosen

Bob was raised in a Scandinavian culture in Minnesota where open displays of emotion among men are frowned upon. This "emotional thriftiness," as someone called it, is seen as a sign of character rather than emotional repression. One comedian familiar with the culture of the Upper Midwest said that if you came across a Scandinavian who had just been drawn and quartered and asked him, "How are you feeling?" he would bravely respond, "Just fair."

Bob served as a pastor amongst this culture for several years, and we were often concerned when we saw grieving family members go through the death of a loved one and never cry. Sadly, such unnatural behavior was often rewarded by other well-meaning people who said, "I can see you're really holding up well," or "It's evident the Lord is giving you strength to get through this," or "It's better this way." (This last comment has always puzzled us. How can it be better that someone you loved is dead rather than alive, healthy, and a loving part of your life?)

Our exhortation to such stoic family members went in the opposite direction: "Don't be afraid to show your grief. To grieve much is to have loved much. Use this time to let your feelings of sorrow out. The more you grieve now, the less you will have to grieve later."

While a wife cannot force her husband to display his emotions, she can encourage him in that direction (again, mainly without words). The goal is not for a man to become as naturally emotive as a woman but for him to feel the freedom, when needed, to get in touch with his heart. If there is buried grief or sorrow there, it will not be resolved until it is expressed in some manner.

Real Men Show Real Emotions

While most men are not wired to be as emotionally expressive or intuitive as women are, it is definitely not unmasculine for a man's man to display his emotions from the heart. Jesus openly wept at the grave of his friend Lazarus. Joseph in Egypt wept at the sight of his brothers after long years of separation. The elders at Ephesus wept as Paul told them they would never see him again. The great men of God in both the Old and New Testament were not ashamed to show their emotions at important moments.

A wife can encourage her husband by patiently, respectfully, and quietly giving him generous time and space to work out his true feelings and emotions. If he does display deep emotion, the best response is to say little or nothing; just hold him and quietly weep with him. That will mean more to him than ten thousand words of comfort.

---

7. Men don't talk because they do not believe they will be listened to.

This brings us back to the basic premise of this book: *There aren't any men who cannot talk, only those who believe they will not be listened to.*

For those of you who believe your husband does not or will not talk to you, there is hope. Your husband has inside him just as many thoughts and convictions as you do. The reasons they go unexpressed may be as many and varied as this chapter has attempted to explain. At the end of the day, every person—male or female—desires to know and be known. We were created for relationships, and even the most aloof husband still has inside a longing to connect on an emotional, spiritual, and physical level with someone.

An Affair: A Sad Stay on Fantasy Island

That is one explanation why some men, seemingly detached and uncommunicative with their wives, become involved in an emotional and physical affair with other women. If they didn't have the need or the capacity to become connected to someone, why would they ever pursue an affair? Even an illicit relationship demands of a man a certain level of communication, vulnerability, and emotional effort. So it's not that men don't desire deep relationships or lack the capacity to communicate feelings and desires; it's that something is blocking them from doing so in their current relationships.

As an aside, men who are emotionally blocked in their marriages eventually find themselves blocked as well in their new fling with the other woman. Affairs are a fantasy fueled by two self-seeking individuals who foolishly believe the answer to their problems is another lover. That's why the vast majority of affairs fizzle out over time, and those that do lead to marriage end in divorce at a statistically higher rate than first marriages.

Once the sexual and romantic high is over, one or both people realize their hearts are still detached, self-focused, and dammed up. They are no more able to build a mutually fulfilling and intimate relationship than they were with their first spouse. Only now the landscape of their lives is littered with family casualties and character wreckage that their self-centered fling produced. Like an Oklahoma tornado that roars through Main Street at midnight, the morning reveals nothing but debris, devastation, and tears.

That's why it's so important that a husband talk to his wife. Maintaining an ongoing emotional connection between their two hearts will nurture love and serve as the very best preventative medicine in warding off an affair.

Love Can Drive a Conversation

Bob was traveling back with eight or so men from a fishing trip to Canada when the group voted to drive through the night. By 11:00 p.m., no one really wanted to drive; they all wanted to sleep. They asked if anyone in the vehicle was willing to take the wheel for the graveyard shift, and a man in his midtwenties eagerly volunteered. With that the others settled down for as much sleep as they could get sitting up in a cargo van.

How did the young man stay awake for the all-night drive? Simple—he called his girlfriend that he was very much in love with. The two of them talked for almost four hours as he cruised down the dark interstate at seventy miles per hour. He finally hung up just as the sun was starting to turn the morning sky shades of red.

Amazing, isn't it? When a couple is young and in love, they can talk for hours and hours and never lose interest. Once a man gets married, why does he retreat to the flat-screen television or his computer in the back office?

Now that we have looked at some of the reasons why men quit talking, we'll look in the next chapter at the most common mistakes wives make in their well-intentioned efforts to get their husband to talk.

Questions to Consider

1. What is the value of applying the advice of James 1:19 in getting a man to talk? How can the three admonitions to be "quick to listen, slow to speak and slow to become angry" change the dynamics of communication between a husband and a wife?

2. Why would the fear of rejection keep a man from talking? Why is it important that wives follow the instructions of Romans 15:7 to "accept one another" in getting their husband to talk? What are some verbal and nonverbal cues of acceptance that you can send to your husband?

3. Would you agree that most wives are more verbally skilled than their husband? Why is it important to follow 1 Peter 3:1 in relating to your husband even if he is a believer? What does it mean to win him without words? Have you ever tried that?

4. What if you had been raised in a home where you were punished for expressing your true feelings? How could that affect your marriage later on? How does Psalm 69:20 speak to such an experience?

5. Do you agree or disagree that "there aren't any men who cannot talk, only those who do not believe they will be listened to"? What is the warning of Proverbs 18:13 when it comes to speaking before listening? Could that be a factor at work in your marriage? On a scale of one to ten, how would you rate yourself as a listener?

2

The Most Common Mistakes Wives Make Trying to Get Their Husbands to Talk

"She who answers before listening—
that is her folly and her shame."

PROVERBS 18:13 (OUR PARAPHRASE)

Recently we were part of a couples' Bible study that gave us a firsthand glimpse into marriage dynamics. One reason the study was so revealing was that the topic was marriage, and it quickly became obvious that many wives had much more to say than did their husbands.

One young couple, newly married, fit a pattern we had seen many times. Heather was outspoken and outgoing, though sometimes a little overbearing. Whatever aspect of marriage we were discussing, she would quickly jump in and share her ideas. Occasionally she would turn to her husband, a soft-spoken and rather shy software engineer, and say, "Dennis, say something. We're all supposed to share." Dennis would blush, look around the room as if desperately searching for his thoughts (or the exit), and eventually mumble something like, "Heather's right."

Miss Perfect Meets Mr. Right—Does It Get Any Better?

It became painfully clear as the weeks wore on that one of Heather's reasons for attending the study was to "fix" Dennis. She was hoping the Bible study would convict him of his need to be as assertive, verbal, and romantic a player in their marriage as she was. It's natural for opposites to attract. High-energy, highly expressive, and apparently confident women are often attracted to shy, more reserved, and slightly more uncertain men (and vice versa). Perhaps both instinctively know that the traits the other person possesses could bring balance to their own lives and personality.

While opposites may attract, they rarely stay attracted. Over time the genuine differences between them move from being charming to curious to distracting to downright annoying. It's at that point a couple usually goes one of two directions: they either try to change each other (which has yet to work in our experience) or they begin moving apart (which has yet to work either). While the strong and silent type may drive a young woman crazy with desire while they are courting or dating, it can drive her nearly over the edge with frustration once they do marry.

In our marriage conference, we often present two singles in their early twenties, the imaginary Miss Perfect and Mr. Right, who have just met. The phone conversations that follow with friends or family members often go like this:

"Jane, this is Megan. I just had to call you and tell you I have met Mr. Right. That's right! He works in the same department as I do and lately he's been texting me during his breaks. They are so sweet and thoughtful. He's also taken me to lunch at the coffee shop across the street. All the other women are sooooo jealous of me. Yes, his name is Kevin, and no, he doesn't say much. But he's deep. He's the strong and silent type. It drives me crazy to be away from him. We've been seeing each other for about two months now. He's invited me to meet his family next weekend. Jane, I think this is it. It may be a little early, but let's start looking at dresses…"

Fast-forward the tape ten years.

"Hello, Jane, this is Megan. Sorry to bother you on a Sunday afternoon, but I just had to talk to someone. The kids are in the other room playing, and I'm just reading the same magazine for the third time. How's Kevin? Oh, he's fine, I guess. He just sits there in front of the TV watching three football games at once. He never says a word. He can go for hours without moving. The other day I had to go over and feel the pulse in his neck to see if he's still with us. I don't know if I can take this much longer…"

Now let's look at this from Mr. Right's perspective. Let's start with the day he calls his dad to tell him he may have met the woman of his dreams:

"Hey, Dad, it's Kevin. Yeah, I'm fine. Yeah, the car's working fine too. Just had the tires rotated and the oil changed. Yeah, the Cubs are in last place again, so what's new? Dad, the reason I'm calling is that I've met this girl. She works in my department. Dad, she's gorgeous. Not only that she talks to everyone—she's like a party in a box. The other day we went out to eat at a restaurant and she knew everyone behind the counter, and they asked her if her cat was feeling better. I don't know, Dad, did you feel this way about Mom when you met her? I've had to beat out some other losers in the office who wanted to date her. But I think she likes me—maybe a lot. Now, please tell Mom not to get her hopes up, but I think I may have found the one…"

Fast-forward the tape ten years.

"Hello, Dad. Yeah, it's me, Kevin. Hope I'm not interrupting the game or anything. I just needed some peace and quiet. It's Megan, Dad—all she does is talk. I mean she talks day and night. She even talks in her sleep. The other day she spent half an hour on a wrong number. Dad, did you ever have to go through this with Mom? I mean, when all you want is to be left alone for a few minutes…"

The truth of the matter is that neither Megan nor Kevin has changed since they got married. They are essentially the same people they were the day they met.

What has changed is how they see each other.

What used to attract them about each other now repels them. What they once found so cute and charming is now aggravating and upsetting. Where they once couldn't wait to be together, they now live essentially separate lives under the same roof.

Three Reasons Things Change After Marriage

So why is it that Kevin and Megan could get along so well when they were dating but find it so difficult to connect now they are married?

How have Miss Perfect and Mr. Right become Mrs. Flaws and Mr. Boring? We suggest at least three reasons.

---

1. While infatuation idealizes the truth, marriage realizes the truth.

Someone once defined *infatuation* as temporary insanity. They weren't far from right. God in his wisdom designed each of us so that, for a brief time, hormones in our body are released that give us those wonderful, dreamy, euphoric feelings of being in love. The writer of the Song of Songs captures these elated and passionate feelings of young love:

> I delight to sit in his shade,
>   and his fruit is sweet to my taste.
> Let him lead me to the banquet hall,
>   and let his banner over me be love.
> Strengthen me with raisins;
>   refresh me with apples,
>   *for I am faint with love.*
> (Songs of Songs 2:3-5, emphasis ours)

Studies show that the same hormones that produce those feelings will eventually wear out. When they do, reality sets in. Once the honeymoon is over and a couple must go about the daily challenges of merging two lives, the flaws and imperfections start to come out.

Should You Throw In the Towel?

Cheryl experienced several shocks just months into our marriage. She had been raised in a home with three sweet sisters and no brothers. She had little exposure to the behavior, thinking, and habits of men other than her father. Bob had been raised with a brother and sisters, and during college he lived in a dorm and then in an apartment with other men. Let's just say his standards of hygiene as an adult single male were not exactly on the same level as Cheryl experienced growing up. Cheryl was surprised, maybe even shocked (okay, we'll admit it—she was traumatized), the first time she saw Bob blow his nose in a bathroom towel.

Once the hormones wear off and reality sets in, it often becomes painfully apparent that many husbands are going to be less verbal, more withdrawn, and will tend to keep their feelings bottled up. Yet the new wife deeply needs conversation and communication with her husband to experience intimacy and emotional connection. When that doesn't happen as she imagined it would, she may become unsettled, unsure, and even desperate in her efforts to fix their marriage.

---

2. The thrill of the sexual chase is over.

The second reason everything that was coming up roses has now become the war of weeds is that single men can act out of character for a season when they are driven by sexual desire. We're not talking about sinful manifestations such as lust or fornication. We're referring to the natural and God-given sexual desires a man has for a woman. When a man falls in love, his sublimated and delayed sexual desires may take on some rather surprising expressions in both his behavior and personality. This pattern continues until he marries.

A Poet Who Didn't Know It

When Bob was dating Cheryl, he began writing her poetry. A few years ago he found the red spiral-bound notebook containing those poems along with other prosaic expressions of his love for Cheryl during those gaga days. Eventually we married…and Bob has not written a line of poetry for nearly three decades. What happened?

Other single men, deeply infatuated, will go to great lengths to set up the perfect engagement. They will have a helicopter land in a park to deliver the diamond ring, or they'll hire an entire string ensemble to appear at their dinner table while he proposes. One poor soul attempted to propose on the court during halftime of an NBA game with thousands watching. The dumbstruck girl at first looked shocked, then shook her head no, and ultimately ran out of the arena in tears, leaving Mr. Don Juan slam-dunked.

The Contented-Bull Theory

Why do many men act as if they have temporarily lost their minds during this season of hyper-infatuation?

Sex.

There. We said it. Now deal with it.

Not that the young man doesn't have genuine interest in the woman he is pursuing. Not that he doesn't share her core values, convictions, and vision for life. Not that he doesn't find her personality engaging and her thoughts challenging. Sure. But why does a shy, somewhat uncreative if not boring person suddenly become "The World's Most Interesting Man" for a season?

Sex.

That's right. It helps explain why once he marries and the thrill of the sexual chase is gone and his physical needs are regularly being met, he then goes back to who he really was all along. In college one of our married friends used to refer to this phenomenon as the "contented-bull theory." Once the man weds and has his sexual needs met, he tends (unfortunately) to return to a focus on career, sports, cars, and other distractions. His new wife, who was at times spellbound by his creativity and tenacity in pursuing her, now looks at a man who seems bored, indifferent, and definitely unromantic.

Why does she feel that way? Because he has quit talking to her. Remembering his passionate poetry, elaborate dates, and nonstop conversation over dinner, she now feels cheated. *Was that all just an act to get me to marry him? Why has he lost interest in me? Is there someone else in his life now?*

The answer to those questions is typically no. But the white-hot jet fuel of his unfulfilled sexual desires, which once propelled him to amazing romantic feats, now burns more like a Coleman camp stove on propane. It can cook a nice dinner, but it rarely heats up the place.

---

3. Unresolved heart damage has built a wall between them.

We wrote an entire book on how a damaged or hardened heart can build a wall between a husband and wife (*The Marriage Miracle: How*

Two Soft Hearts Can Make a Couple Strong, Harvest House Publishers, 2010). We won't rehearse the content of that book other than to say all of us are created in the image of God with hearts able to give and to receive love. As a dear friend and marriage counselor, John Regier, points out in his writings, two things lock up our hearts: *pain* and *sin.*

Pain is the emotional and spiritual injury others cause us, most often during our childhood and adolescence. *Sin* is the choice we make in response to pain that can further harden our hearts and prevent us from being able to give and to receive love.

An unresolved heart issue is the primary reason why husbands won't talk to their wives and why wives can be reluctant to engage in physical intimacy with their husbands. These are among the most common problems we encounter in our ministry to couples.

Taking Inventory of Your Heart

The healing of heart issues involves diagnosing what type of hardened heart we may have (there are at least twelve varieties). To help with this diagnosis, we have compiled "A Personal Heart Exam" that you may wish to take to see what type of hardened heart you may have brought to your marriage. (You'll find the exam in the appendix at the back of the book.)

As we have discussed so far in this book, underlying emotional and spiritual issues often hinder a husband from talking and sharing his feelings. That's why if a wife will show her husband love, respect, and patience and allow him to talk about his life and struggles, those heart issues may well surface.

Once a wife begins to show care for her husband's heart pain, is willing to walk with him on the road to forgiving those who created it, and prays with him for Jesus's healing in his life, his heart can change. When his heart changes, chances are he will start talking.

The promises of Scripture are amazing when it comes to God's desire to heal our damaged hearts. Listen to God's beautiful words of promise to cleanse and restore the defiled and scattered nation of Israel: "I will give you a new heart and put a new spirit in you; I will remove from you your heart of stone and give you a heart of flesh" (Ezekiel

36:26). We believe this promise remains applicable today for those of us who have experienced the new birth in Christ.

The Common Mistakes Wives Make

While both husband and wife may bear responsibility for the growing distance in their marriage, this book focuses on how to get a reluctant husband to talk freely and openly with his wife. With that in mind, let's look at the five most frequent mistakes wives can make in trying to get their husband to talk.

---

1. Wives make a mistake when they pressure their husband for an immediate response.

"So are we ready to tell our daughter she cannot date Jeff any longer?"

"Tell me why you're never willing to stand up for yourself with your boss."

"How do you feel our marriage has changed over the last ten years?"

These are all important matters a wife may sincerely want to discuss with her husband. But if she insists that he respond here and now, even before they leave the dinner table, she will likely be disappointed.

Many men go quiet and shut down when confronted with a difficult and complex emotional question—particularly when they are unsure of the answer. Their silence is not so much an act of defiance or disinterest as it is simply an expression of uncertainty. Rather than risk saying something he might later have to walk back, apologize for, or appear stupid for saying, he will likely opt to say nothing.

Following the Advice of Groucho Marx

Men often live by the familiar proverb, "Better to say nothing and be thought a fool than to open your mouth and remove all doubt." While no one knows with certainty who first uttered that colloquial wisdom (Mark Twain, Abraham Lincoln, and Groucho Marx have all been suggested), that person was speaking the philosophy of a great number of men. The writer of Proverbs agrees with this cautious approach:

Even fools are thought wise if they keep silent,
and discerning if they hold their tongues.
(Proverbs 17:28)

It's vital that a wife remember that when she asks her husband a question that requires him to address his feelings, emotions, or relationships, *he will need time to process.* If a wife pressures her husband for an immediate response, she can often expect a disappointing result. Though she may interpret his hesitancy as stubbornness, disinterest, or defiance, he simply needs time to think about his response rather than say something wrong or even stupid.

Consider looking at this phenomenon as something of a compliment. The fact he hesitates with his answer is an indication he considers what you've said such an important question, he would rather take the time to think about it rather than give you a flippant or superficial response.

Give Him Time and Space

A wife who wants her husband's opinion on an important matter, such as family relationships, is far better served by presenting him the issue with an open-ended timeline. Here's an example of what we mean:

"Dear, our daughter is showing all the signs of becoming too emotionally involved with Jeff. Her grades are slipping, she's spending hour after hour texting him, and she even missed youth group last Sunday night to talk to him on the phone. I know you two have a good relationship, so please, just think about how we can address this before things get out of hand."

Such a nonthreatening approach to a difficult problem gives her husband the needed time and space to work through his thoughts. Unless he is truly detached from the family, which sadly some men are, he will likely respond, "Let me think about how I want to approach her on this and I'll get back to you." He will likely keep his word, and in a day or two or three, share with you his ideas and what he intends to do about it.

Only now he has the confidence of knowing what he thinks.

Brain Bridges and the Great Divide

As we mentioned in the first chapter, there may be a physiological/ neurological explanation behind this phenomenon of men requiring time to process complex emotional and relational issues. Researchers have discovered that boys in the womb are given a bath of the male hormone testosterone at a critical point that alters the function of their brain. As a result, numerous connecting links between the two halves of the male brain are altered and communication between the two halves is now much more difficult. The female is born with significantly more connecting bridges between the two halves of her brain that allow her to quickly process emotional and relational data back and forth.

This may be one explanation for the verbal, emotional, and relational advantages most women have over most men. It can also explain why men are more comfortable playing catch rather than ping-pong when it comes to conversation.

We are in no way suggesting that men are born with inferior intellectual abilities compared to women. But when it comes to the innate ability to quickly understand, clarify, and articulate their emotions and feelings, women may possess the natural advantage.

To repeat the takeaway for wives trying to get their husbands to talk: rather than demand an immediate response from your husband to your questions and concerns, offer him an open-ended timeline. By taking the pressure off him to say something right now, it is far more likely he will think about the question and get back to you with his answer when he is prepared to do so.

Name, Rank, and the Green Bay Packers

Men are famous for their ability to resist interrogation. One of the true heroes of the Vietnam War was an American POW interrogated on camera by his captors for propaganda purposes. They demanded that he give them right now the names and ranks of the pilots in his squadron. He complied by giving them a list of names—the starting lineup of the Green Bay Packers: "Captain Bart Starr, Lieutenant Ray Nitschke…" Americans everywhere cheered this man's brilliant defiance while his captors proudly strutted around, believing they had scored an enormous propaganda victory.

When men don't want to talk, you can't force them.

That's why a wife, desperate to receive emotional support, may turn up the pressure to get her husband to talk right now. After all, doesn't her sister talk with her for hours on end over a cup of coffee at Starbucks? But her husband is not her sister, and he will talk to her when he is ready, not before.

---

2. Wives make a mistake when they assume men enjoy conversation just as much as they do.

One of the ways we illustrate at marriage conferences the innate differences between men and women when it comes to conversation is the following announcement Bob makes about Men's Day at their church. He usually says something like this:

"Men, I'm planning one of the most awesome, incredible, and memorable days of your life. Forget your tickets to the next college game or that you were planning to go hunting with your brother-in-law. I'm offering you something that will make those activities pale in comparison.

"Next Saturday I want you to arrive at the church at 7:30 a.m. We've rented three buses to take us all to the largest Starbucks in town, and for the next six hours, we're all going to sit in a large circle and share. Are you ready to rumble with a fresh latte?"

There is usually silence in the room. Dead silence. For men, spending an entire day at Starbucks in a large circle sharing their feelings is not a dream come true; it's more a nightmare they can't wake up from. Bob continues his illustration:

"I know what you're thinking, men. I can see it on your faces. But what if I were put in charge of Women's Day for next Saturday? What if I got up and announced to all the wives of the church that next weekend we husbands will give all of you the day off? We'll watch the kids, do the chores at home, and even make supper. Furthermore, we've rented three buses that will carry you to the largest Starbucks in the area and we've paid the tab in advance. You can order whatever coffee or pastries you want.

"Not only that but you'll be free to sit in groups of two or three and just talk for the entire day. One of you can talk at a time or two of you can talk at one time—shucks you can all talk at once if you wish. A verbal tsunami can wash over the room.

"I have a feeling that at the end of the day, the wives would return home and say, 'That was one of the very best days I've had in a long time. Could we have a day like that at the church next month, Sweetheart?'"

Words Are Little Pieces of a Woman's Soul

What just happened here?

Men are ready to run for the hills and form survivalist groups rather than spend a day of forced "sharing" in a large circle with other men. Yet the women said this was one of the best days of their lives. It's because words are little pieces of a woman's soul. They are the coin of their heart. They are the connecting points that allow them to feel understood and cared for with others. Words are everything to a woman.

But to a man, words are simply a means of communicating information and gathering data. Men are far more affected by actions than syllables. Ask your husband who he admired most growing up, and he will likely tell you about a coach who believed in him, or a father who took him fishing, or a grandmother who made him his favorite pie each time he visited her.

Men will tell you they admired what someone did much more often than what someone said.

Actions Are Louder than Words to Men

Therein lies a basic difference between men and women (again, we realize for every rule there are exceptions). While women find fulfillment in words, men more often find fulfillment in actions. That helps explain why so many men are reluctant to talk and so many women are so eager. That's why men often believe their actions should speak for themselves to their wives.

"Why do I need to say I love you? Don't I go to work each day to provide for our family, then come home and pay bills and keep the cars going, and then remain completely faithful to you? If these aren't statements of love, what is?"

That's why husbands are often deeply hurt when their wives accuse them of not loving them because they don't say "I love you" as often as the wives wish they would.

Bob usually brings closure to this illustration of the differences between men and women by telling the men what he would do if he truly were in charge of Men's Day:

"Guys, I will urge all of you to give up your tickets to the game, or forego the opening of bow-hunting season, or leave your boat in the driveway next Saturday by offering you just one word: *food*.

"That's right—if I'm in charge of Men's Day, I will make it about food. We'll broil, bake, steam, grill, fry, stew, barbecue...whatever it takes to make mouthwatering ribs, barbecued brisket, fried chicken, grilled bratwurst, seared steak, pulled pork, sliced ham, fried hamburgers, broiled fish, and more. These will just be the main course. For side dishes we'll offer baked beans, corn on the cob, coleslaw, baked macaroni and cheese, hot biscuits, cornbread, hash browns, black-eyed peas, bacon-flavored green beans, french fries, and that's just for starters. All of you can eat until you fall over in your chair. At that point we'll provide people to help you sit up again so you have room for dessert.

"Following lunch, we'll divide you into two teams. We'll assign you work projects around the church, and the team that finishes first with the highest quality will receive a five-foot-seven trophy. No doubt while you're working there will be good-natured banter. You'll occasionally yell things at each other like, 'Hey, are you working hard or hardly working?' To which the other team will respond, 'Who are you calling lazy? You're so ugly the day you were born the doctor slapped your mother.'

"Now really, men, if we had Men's Day at the church and you were given all the food you could eat, had tough competition that handed out enormous trophies, and you could toss harmless insults at each other all day, who wouldn't show up?"

By that time almost every man in the room is smiling and nodding in approval.

The truth is, most men don't enjoy conversation as much as women do. They are drawn, however, to activity (particularly eating). Wives make a big mistake (and an erroneous assumption) when they believe men find as much fulfillment in talking as they do. Men are willing to talk, but as we will see later, it usually has to be under the right conditions.

---

3. Wives make a mistake when they don't understand men talk as the result of an activity, whereas women see talking as the activity itself.

That thought is by no means original with us. We first came across it in an article by Dr. Lois Davidtz in a women's magazine. The female psychologist who studied differences between the sexes concluded, "Men talk as the result of doing an activity. Women see it as the activity itself."

That brief insight proved to be an enormous asset in helping us understand how to get men to talk to their wives. It also explains why so many men squirm while their wives are trying to get a deep and probing conversation started. Women would rather talk just to talk, but men will talk only if they are already doing something else.

A Healthy Case of the Shingles

Bob first experienced this principle at work when he was in college and worked summers roofing houses with his father, a well-educated math teacher who was also a decorated pilot from World War II. Yet Bob's dad, like many men from the Greatest Generation, preferred to say less about their wartime experiences and concentrate on fulfilling their duties as a husband, father, and provider.

As a result Bob's dad said little about his life or experiences and certainly nothing about his feelings. Bob's mother, a full-blooded Swede and an extrovert, was born to talk.

What Bob learned of his father's personal life came primarily from the five summers they spent together roofing houses (truly a gift from God). Sitting on top of an asphalt roof some twenty feet in the air, under a blazing summer sun and ninety-degree temperatures, covered from head to foot with shingle granules and black roofing cement, an amazing thing occurred.

Bob's dad began to talk.

As they carried sixty-pound bundles up two or even three stories on a ladder, as they handed one another chalk lines and shingle nails, as they molded aluminum flashing around chimneys and sewer vents, Bob's dad began to say things.

He talked about his years growing up on the dusty plains of western North Dakota. He talked about his dear mother who died of rheumatic fever when he was only seventeen—and how he vowed at her graveside never to disgrace her. He talked about how he volunteered at twenty years of age to become a pilot in the Army Air Corps and flew countless dangerous missions over southern Europe. He fought back tears as he recounted the loss of comrades whose planes spiraled downward in a blaze of smoke and fire after being hit by antiaircraft guns. He talked about returning home to discover that the farm now belonged to his brother. He talked about going to college on the GI Bill and driving out of the driveway towing a trailer containing all his possessions to attend school.

Yes, Bob's dad talked on and on about things Bob knew little about. He learned more about his father during those five summers high atop a roof than all the previous eighteen years that he had sat at the dinner table with his father.

What happened to turn his father from Secret Sam into one of the World's Most Interesting Men?

Men talk when they're doing something.

Dr. Davidtz was right: "Men talk as the result of an activity while women see it as the activity itself." A wife need not despair because her husband doesn't enjoy talking as much as she does. The answer may lie in finding an activity they both enjoy and doing that together each day.

We'll talk more about this in a later chapter, but the takeaway for now is that a wife should give up (in most cases) believing that her husband finds fulfillment talking as much as she does. He will talk, but it will typically be when he's engaged in some activity rather than sitting across the table as you stare into each other's eyes.

---

4. Wives make a mistake when they interrupt, evaluate, or criticize their husband's thoughts as soon as he shares them.

At the risk of repeating ourselves, there is perhaps nothing a wife can do that will get her husband to quit talking more quickly (and perhaps for good) than to immediately react in a negative way to his thoughts or ideas.

Why Men Go on Strike

Men operate by something of a three-strike rule. "I'll give you one chance to hear what I say, I'll give you two chances to hear what I think, but if I share myself a third time and you reject or critique what I say, that's it. I'm not going to say anything else." To some extent, women see conversation as a chance to sharpen each other's thoughts and ideas by immediately responding to them—even by vigorously disagreeing or rejecting the person's statement altogether.

However, when men share their thoughts and ideas and they are immediately criticized or rejected, it's more like a sword has been thrust through them. Their sense of dignity and self-respect feels wounded when they hear statements such as, "I have no idea how you could think that way," or "You are absolutely forgetting what happened last month," or "I couldn't disagree with you more."

While the wife may respond in these ways in order to clarify the issues and ultimately reach common ground (a frequent female goal), the husband believes she obviously thinks she's right and he's wrong.

At that point, he decides whether to get into an argument or simply be quiet and let her have her way.

Men usually respond well when they are given an opportunity to talk without being interrupted, evaluated, or criticized (at least right at the moment). It explains why a man who doesn't say fifty words to his wife at home will spend two and a half hours telling his life story at our office. In the first environment, he may feel he is going to be evaluated or judged; in the second setting, he believes his thoughts will be accepted and listened to in a nonjudgmental manner. (That's our intention, at least.)

In trying to heal a hurting marriage where the dynamics are a strong and talkative wife who's matched with a more tentative and quiet husband, we strongly suggest the wife practice simply listening and affirming her husband's words. She doesn't have to be dishonest and say she agrees when she doesn't. But she can offer such encouraging statements as, "Thank you for telling me your thoughts," "I can honestly see how you would feel that way," or "I respect how you feel about this."

Back in our college days, one of the clichés everyone was using was "Stifle yourself." It was another way of saying, you don't have to say everything that comes into your mind. Some relationships can move forward only if a wife practices patience and self-control in responding to the thoughts and ideas of her spouse.

Why He Stuffs His Stuff

Sadly, if a husband believes his thoughts or ideas will be immediately held up to scrutiny and criticism, he will shut up rather than face the jury. The more he stuffs his thoughts and ideas, the more likely resentment will grow toward his wife.

As his frustration and anger grow, it is more likely they will come out sideways. He may become passive-aggressive in his behavior. One husband would put on his headphones and listen to his iPod. He may pretend not to hear when his wife asks him something. He may interject sarcasm into his words. He may refer to her as "the boss" behind her back. While counterproductive responses, they are also not-so-subtle signals he feels disrespected and walked on.

The possibility also exists that one day he will flip and go from one end of the emotional spectrum to the other. From a passive teddy bear, he turns into an aggressive and angry grizzly. His temperament becomes overtly hostile, he walks around with a hair-trigger temper, and he criticizes his wife openly in front of the children.

Or the possibility exists he will turn all his anger inward and sink into depression or find himself in bondage to various addictions. The pain that's driving all his negative behavior can likely be traced back to painful childhood experiences. Perhaps it was an overbearing father or mother who sent the message loud and clear, "I don't care what you think. You're not that important. I'm the important one in this family, so sit down and shut up."

An Explanation, Not an Excuse, for Addictive Behavior

As one marriage counselor says, this husband may be outwardly complying with his wife's decisions but inwardly he's reacting to them. Such a man is a setup for addictive behaviors, including pornography, overeating, drinking and drugs, and sadly, eventually looking for another woman.

Dante and his wife, Rachelle, were having serious marriage problems. When they met with us, it was clear she had no problem expressing her feelings and opinions. Her main complaint was that her husband had simply checked out of the marriage. "He sits for hours in front of the television and says nothing," she said. "When I try to engage him, he either just ignores me or turns up the volume, leaving me in tears."

As we listened to Dante's life story, we discovered that his father was a dominant, often violent man whose discipline frequently turned into physical abuse. Dante grew up learning to stay quiet and clear of his father's leather belt. What's worse is that his dad was a pastor who appeared calm and gentle to others. The emotional inventory tests he took showed he could now neither assert nor express himself—except when he was angry. His depression had worsened to the point where he had not worked for almost six months. Their financial situation was rapidly becoming dire.

"What do you think your father's anger and abuse did to your heart?" we asked. We just sat and listened, offering neither critique nor rebuttal, as Dante began to express feelings that had been kept inside for decades.

The next time we met, Dante said, "You know, I never realized how much my father's treatment of me is an issue in my life." Tears welled up in his eyes and he began to weep. "I just never thought about it much. Now I can see how much it impacted me." He shook his head as he struggled to regain his composure.

Rachelle began to see a side of her husband she had never seen before. Underneath his passive-aggressive anger, which she had endured for so many years, was the heart of a young boy who was just scared of his father. His dad's abuse had served to tear the clutch out of his soul. That's why he couldn't make decisions or keep a job and had basically given up on life. He had lost the sense of being a person—particularly a person of value.

Wisely, Rachelle said little as Dante continued to pour out his heart. But her occasional loving look of sorrow or gesture of compassion was starting to make an impact. She began to reach out to him and care for the hurts in his heart.

As Dante began to discover he could assert his thoughts and feelings without incurring someone's wrath, you could see the change in his countenance. Little by little he started smiling again and becoming more talkative.

"What would be a dream job for you?" we asked. (Such positive, nonthreatening questions can be used to help men open up and share their dreams and aspirations for life.)

"I've always wanted to open my own computer store," he said.

"Why don't you?"

"I don't know if anyone would want to invest in me..."

Dante's lifelong lack of confidence started to seep out again, but this time he caught himself. He realized it was okay to have dreams for the future—that's part of being a person. At the same time his wife was learning how important it was to just let him talk without critiquing or rejecting his thoughts.

Dante's father should have been the first one to draw out his son's true feelings and dreams, but sadly he had done just the opposite. The Bible describes the proper role of a father in 1 Thessalonians 2:11-12: "For you know that we dealt with each of you as a father deals with his own children, encouraging, comforting and urging you to live lives worthy of God, who calls you into his kingdom and glory."

By the way, Dante wrote us about a year later to say he had opened a computer store.

---

5. Wives make a mistake when they become uncomfortable with dead air and try to fill the awkward silence.

One day after we had done an interview at a radio station, an alarm suddenly went off. Employees began scurrying toward a large bank of audio equipment mounted on the wall.

"How long has this been going on?" one radio engineer said urgently.

"I don't know," said another in a worried voice. "Maybe a minute or two."

What was the crisis? A fire alarm? A security breach? No, it was something every radio station dreads—"dead air." That's when a technical glitch occurs and suddenly no audio is being broadcast. For those tuned to the station, it's "The Sounds of Silence," as Simon and Garfunkel's 1960's hit song puts it. There's nothing...nada...and that's deadly to a radio station that makes its living by providing meaningful sounds to people.

Does Your Husband Sing "The Sounds of Silence"?

In a similar fashion an alarm may go off inside a wife's heart when there is dead air in the conversation between her and her husband. Typically females, due to their innate desire to nurture and protect, will jump in to fill the dead air by saying something, anything, just so the situation doesn't become awkward.

"Well, maybe what you're struggling with is…"

"You know I once faced a similar situation and what I learned…"

"I suppose we could just talk about this another time…"

All these statements are usually intended to spare the husband embarrassment because he appears not to know what to say next. It's an attempt to salvage the conversation and keep the dialogue sailing along.

It's exactly the wrong thing to do with men.

As hard as it may be for a wife to believe, dead air is not a personal or emotional threat to a man's self-image or dignity. In fact, it's just a man being a man. Men often take long pauses in their conversation with one another to consider what's just been said or what they may say in response. It's the equivalent of letting a marathon runner catch his breath so he can pick up and continue his long course. It allows men time to gather their thoughts before they get back in the game.

Unfortunately, when wives instinctively jump in to fill dead air, the result is usually the opposite of what she had hoped for. Instead of reengaging, her husband may go quiet and eventually choose to end the conversation. He's now feeling pressured, squelched, or overwhelmed by his mate's insistence that there be words constantly going back and forth. We suggest that when dead air occurs in a conversation, a wife should simply relax and smile at her husband and wait for him to say something.

The Difference Between a Comma and a Period

But what if the silence goes on for fifteen seconds, thirty seconds, or even ten minutes? That can feel like an eternity to a woman who is used to playing ping-pong. To respond effectively, a wife will need to adjust her thinking from a female perspective to a male one.

For most men, dead air is no more an enemy of conversation than a comma is an enemy of a sentence. It is simply a pause, often a pregnant pause, because during that interlude, a man is preparing to give birth to more ideas, thoughts, and conversation.

We're told by salespeople that when they make "the ask" in an attempted sale, the first person to speak always loses. That's why they will stay absolutely quiet until the customer responds first. If the silence is broken first by the salesperson, the customer's typical answer will be no.

If a wife wants a conversation with her husband to continue once she asks a question, she should say nothing—nothing—nothing—until he responds. Trust us, it may take a while, but he will eventually say something. What he eventually says may not be what you hoped for or on the topic you wish he'd discuss, but he will say something. And as long as you choose to essentially remain quiet after he has finally said something, he will likely say more.

The Scriptures attribute virtue to silence in certain settings,

> Sin is not ended by multiplying words,
>   but the prudent hold their tongues.
>   (Proverbs 10:19)

Another version of the Bible puts it this way, "When there are many words, sin is unavoidable" (HCSB). The Bible suggests there is a time to keep quiet, and when we do, it is a sign of prudence and wisdom. It also warns us of the danger of jumping in too quickly:

> To answer before listening—
>   that is folly and shame.
>   (Proverbs 18:13)

This could not be truer when it comes to trying to get your husband to talk. It is absolutely vital that a wife listen before she says something, even during dead air.

Dead Air and the Patience of Job

One of the more powerful examples in Scripture of how effective and redemptive silence can be is found in the book of Job. Many scholars believe Job was the first of the sixty-six books of Scripture to be written. The ancient story chronicles the mysterious and heartbreaking events that turned Job's life from honor, prosperity, and a loving family to a place of disgrace, deprivation, and bereavement. Few men have suffered so much so quickly with no apparent reason as did poor Job.

When word comes to Job's friends that the bottom of his life has fallen out, they drop everything and rush to comfort their anguished friend:

> When Job's three friends, Eliphaz the Temanite, Bildad the Shuhite and Zophar the Naamathite, heard about all the troubles that had come upon him, they set out from their homes and met together by agreement to go and sympathize with him and comfort him. When they saw him from a distance, they could hardly recognize him; they began to weep aloud, and they tore their robes and sprinkled dust on their heads (Job 2:11-12).

What could they say to their heartbroken and physically disfigured friend that would bring him comfort? The Bible tells us, "Then they sat on the ground with him for seven days and seven nights. No one said a word to him, because they saw how great his suffering was" (2:13).

Seven days without a word—that has to be the all-time record for dead air in conversation. But note that Job's three male friends instinctively understood this was no time for words. No, the only way to comfort their poor beleaguered friend was simply to sit with him in total silence.

If only they had stayed that course, the book of Job might have gone a different direction. Instead, Job breaks the silence (see, it works to wait for the man to say something eventually). He pours out his pain and lament to his friends. Rather than stifling themselves and letting Job simply talk on, one of his friends jumps in:

> Then Eliphaz the Temanite replied:
> "If someone ventures a word with you, will you be
>   impatient?
> But who can keep from speaking?"
>   (Job 4:1-2)

What follows are thirty or more chapters of eloquent, well-intentioned, passionate speeches by his friends—all an utter waste in terms of ministering to Job. They squander a precious opportunity to reach and comfort the heart of Job because they cannot resist...talking. They break the dead air and ramble on and on and on, assuming they know the real reason for Job's horrendous suffering—he must have some great sin in his life. If he will only confess and repent of it, then God will restore his fortunes.

Not only are their attempts off the mark, they are offensive to God. In the final chapter of Job we are told:

> After the LORD had said these things to Job, he said to Eliphaz the Temanite, "I am angry with you and your two friends, because you have not spoken the truth about me, as my servant Job has...My servant Job will pray for you, and I will accept his prayer and not deal with you according to your folly..."
> After Job had prayed for his friends, the LORD restored his fortunes and gave him twice as much as he had before (Job 42:7-8,10).

As a wife there may be certain times when you need to speak a word of advice or even rebuke to your husband. But the time to do that is usually not when he is in intense pain or suffering or grief. The best thing to do in such times is simply sit with him, hold his hand, and let him see the love in your eyes.

Job is a profound case in point of the dangers of filling in dead air and speaking too soon. While long and extended pauses may feel awkward for a wife, they are often a refreshing and welcome break during which a husband can gather his thoughts. To him it's a sign of respect that you are willing to wait until he is ready to say something.

Conclusion

For the purpose of review, wives make a mistake in talking to their husbands when:

- They pressure their husband for an immediate response.

- They assume men enjoy conversation just as much as they do.

- They don't understand that men talk as the result of an activity, whereas women see talking as the activity itself.

- They interrupt, evaluate, or criticize their husband's thoughts as soon as he shares them.

- They are uncomfortable with dead air and try to fill in the awkward silence.

In the next chapter we'll look at the types of questions a wife can ask her husband that will encourage him to share his thoughts and ideas with her. Just as in building sexual intimacy a husband needs to understand the need for physical foreplay, in building toward conversational intimacy a wife needs to understand her husband's need for conversational foreplay.

Questions to Consider

1. Do you agree that opposites sometimes attract but then later repel? According to Song of Songs 4:1-16, should our unique differences as men and women bring joy or irritation to our relationship? How do you view the differences between the two of you?

2. How can unresolved heart damage interfere with our ability to talk to one another in open and constructive ways? In Matthew 19.1-8, what did Jesus say is the primary reason Moses permitted divorce in the Old Testament? If two hardened hearts build walls in a marriage, what will two softened hearts do?

3. Why is it a mistake for wives to expect an immediate answer from their husbands? Consider the story found in John 8:1-8. Did Jesus always give an immediate answer? Why do you

think he took time before giving a reply? Is there value in a man carefully weighing his answer before offering it?

4. Would you agree that men talk as the result of an activity while women see talking as the activity itself? How can incorporating that truth into your marriage work to draw out your husband? What is the significance of Jesus holding a conversation with the two men as they were walking on the road to Emmaus (Luke 24:13-16)? Are you willing to try a simple walk with your husband each night?

5. Why are wives often uncomfortable or worry about dead air in a conversation with their husbands? What are some of the virtues of allowing silence that Scripture teaches us? (See Job 13:13; Habakkuk 2:20; Proverbs 10:19.) Why is it a show of respect and honor to allow a man all the time he needs to respond?

3

Seven Questions to Ask Your Husband to Get Him to Talk

"The purposes of a man's heart are deep waters,
but a (wife) who has insight draws them out."

<small>Proverbs 20:5 (our paraphrase)</small>

We were once having problems with a car trunk not closing properly, so Bob took the car to a local body shop. When he entered the repair shop, he was surprised to be confronted by a purebred Great Dane. The dog walked up to sniff Bob's leg, creating a moment of some temporary unease. The Great Dane must have concluded Bob was okay as he eventually turned away, found a rope toy to chew on, and settled down to resume a dog's life.

When the owner came in, Bob casually said, "Is that your dog? It's a nice one. Unfortunately, I had to put down my own dog recently. Losing a good dog is tough, isn't it?"

The owner stared at Bob for a long time and then sat down. "My wife and I have had six Great Danes in our marriage. I've had to put down five of them." He then went on to list all the dog's names, the causes of their illnesses, and how many years each had been with their family. Bob just nodded and listened.

The owner talked on for the next forty-five minutes and ended up moving away from talking about his dog to telling Bob about his daughter, his back injury, his ailing wife, and a host of other topics.

Finally, Bob had to politely interrupt and ask if he could give him an estimate for the cost of repairing the trunk. The owner, realizing time had gotten away from him, typed some information into his computer. When the printer spit out the estimate, the man said, "I'm giving you a break on these parts." It turned out to be a several hundred dollar discount, partly in appreciation for Bob's willingness to listen to him talk about his favorite subject—his Great Dane dogs.

Is there a lesson here? Yes. *If you ask a man the right questions, he will talk.*

And if you continue to listen to him talk with patience, focus, and empathy, he will continue to talk...and talk...and talk. Now imagine if Bob had walked into the store, pulled up to the owner's desk, and said, "Hey, you don't know me, but I'd like to ask you a number of personal questions and have you tell me about your family problems. I've only got a few minutes so let's start talking." Do you think the man would have opened his life to Bob—at least right away? Not likely.

In getting a man to talk, it's vital that you start with questions he is comfortable talking about rather than the ones you are comfortable talking about.

Conversational Foreplay

We realize this next analogy could be awkward, but we believe it reflects the truth about part of God's design to make males and females different from one another. Many wives have long desired for their husbands to understand the vital place of foreplay in preparing them to engage in sexual intimacy. One of the most common complaints wives have is, "He is so eager to reach the main event for him that he doesn't take the time to bring me along with him." The end result is that often the husband has his needs met, but his wife is left frustrated and unfulfilled.

In a similar manner, your husband requires conversational foreplay in order to respond to your desire for a deeper discussion.

Wives often are overly eager to get right to the heart of deeply felt emotions when talking with their husbands. They don't realize that men need to be brought along slowly to the point where they finally feel comfortable engaging in intimate conversation. If a wife starts a conversation in an emotionally safe and nonpressurized manner, she will have more success in getting her husband to talk.

Seven Questions that Can Reach His Heart

One place to begin is by learning to ask good questions of your husband. Let's look at seven questions (topics or categories) that men typically respond to positively. While countless others could be used as well, these seven are illustrative of questions that can get your husband to talk.

Question 1: "What is the most fulfilling aspect of your job?" (Topic: Core Competencies)

Listen to a conversation between two women waiting for their children to complete their piano lesson. More often than not, it will work its way toward relationship issues. "How is your child getting along with the other students?" "What are you doing to help them cope with peer pressure?" "How is your child handling the stress of an afternoon sport?"

Now listen in on a conversation between two men waiting to pick up their kids. Chances are if they aren't talking sports or politics, they'll talk work. "How's business in this economy?" "What are customers asking for these days?" "How are new government regulations affecting your profits?"

Why are men talking about work while women are talking about kids? Women draw much of their identity from their relationships while men draw much of their identity from their occupation. If that's the case, then wouldn't it make sense to begin a conversation with your husband by asking him about his work, such as, "What's the most fulfilling aspect of your job?"

Because men often possess confidence in talking about their core competence, asking questions about their livelihood is a great starting place for a conversation.

We once visited a friend in the South who makes fine carpets for a living. We asked him one or two questions about how such amazing products are produced, and the next thing we knew we were getting a guided tour of the business. He took almost an hour to introduce us to each worker, explain how long they had been with the company, and what exactly they each did at their station.

Unless a man is completely miserable in his job, there are few topics he will enjoy talking about more than his work. But be sure to start with the positive aspects of his career. Ask him what he enjoys most in what he does for a living, and then be prepared. You could be in for a ten to forty-five minute monologue as the man waxes on about his livelihood.

A listening wife will learn not only how water is purified at the city filtration plant, or how futures are bought and sold on the commodities market, or what it's like to have filled a twenty-four-hour shift at the firehouse—she will start to hear her husband's heart.

A Wife Becomes a Motivational Seeker

It's in the context of a husband discussing his life's work that a wife can begin to understand what motivates him. She will learn about the values he brings to work, the quality of his relationships with coworkers, and what vocational dreams may still be unfulfilled in his life.

Solomon, the author of Ecclesiastes, was eager to describe his work and the satisfaction it brought to him:

> I undertook great projects: I built houses for myself and planted vineyards. I made gardens and parks and planted all kinds of fruit trees in them. I made reservoirs to water groves of flourishing trees...I also owned more herds and flocks than anyone in Jerusalem before me. I amassed silver and gold for myself, and the treasure of kings and provinces...I became greater by far than anyone in Jerusalem before me. In all this my wisdom stayed with me.

> I denied myself nothing my eyes desired;
>> I refused my heart no pleasure.
> My heart took delight in all my labor,
>> and this was the reward for all my toil.
>> (Ecclesiastes 2:4-10)

By letting your husband talk about his work, you will also learn about his core competencies. These competencies—the things he does or knows the most about—typically find expression in a man's vocation or career. That's why he's willing, even eager, to talk about them.

Again, remembering the need for conversational foreplay, it's wise to move slowly into more searching questions about his work. For example, it isn't a good idea to start with questions such as, "Are you worried about losing your job?" "Do you and your boss get along?" "How did your last performance review go?" That's too much, too soon.

How's the Water Today?

Men by nature tend to avoid unpleasant conversations. They need to know the water is safe before they dive into the deep end of a conversation.

Of course men possess core competencies outside the workplace. Your husband may have hobbies, sports, or avocations that allow him to express what he's good at. Besides his career, he may be active in politics, repair vehicles, hunt deer, attend veteran's organizations, garden, participate in sports, and the list goes on. These too are all fruitful areas for starting a discussion as long as you begin in a positive and nonthreatening fashion.

As we said in the previous chapter, Bob's late father was a World War II veteran and the quintessential quiet male. He rarely spoke unless spoken to. Yet, each year when a historical aviation group flew vintage World War II aircraft into town for an air show, Bob's father came alive. He would go out to the airport early in the morning (even in his eighties) where the planes were on display and volunteer to give guided tours of the aircraft to perfect strangers.

He would grin from ear to ear as he described the oxygen tank system, the manual braking system in case of damage to the aircraft, and the approximate weight of the plane when fully loaded with fuel. He would endure the blazing sun of a shadeless runway just for the opportunity to explain his role as a copilot to anyone interested enough to listen. On the tarmac he was in his glory because he was smack-dab in the middle of his core competency.

A wife should never underestimate the wealth of information she will gain about her husband's motivation and values if she will simply ask about, and then listen to, her husband's core competencies. The longer she listens, the more likely she will find the hook that will draw him into conversation on subjects of more interest to her.

The Reason Small-Town Diners Thrive

If you don't believe men love to talk about what they know or do best, just visit a small-town diner or breakfast place about nine on any given morning. Once their early morning chores are done, farmers and other small-town laborers typically take time for coffee or breakfast. Up to eight men will sit around vinyl-topped tables and porcelain white mugs of steaming coffee. Typically wearing baseball caps, overalls, and well-worn jackets bearing the logo of a farm implement or seed company, they lean back and talk about corn prices, machinery repairs, and the lousy weather.

There's a lesson in the small-town diner for wives wishing to get their husbands to talk: *If you let men discuss what they know or do best, they will show up to talk time and again.*

Question 2: "Who is the one person you admire most and why?" (Topic: Core Values)

Men by nature love heroes. Just look at the sales of comic books. Which gender do you think buys the most comic books that feature Spiderman, Iron Man, the Fantastic Four, the Avengers, and Batman? We guarantee you it's not females.

While a young boy or teenager is enthralled by action, clever plot-lines, and stunning graphics, what keeps them coming back for more are the core values of their heroes.

Men Are Drawn to Comic Belief

Bruce Wayne, aka Batman, is driven by a desire to bring justice to street criminals and to protect society from those who would wantonly harm innocent people. The backstory to his ongoing crusade (he's referred to as the Caped Crusader) is the murder of his parents by a street thug when Bruce was young. He exemplifies a male's innate sense of justice and willingness to sacrifice to see it accomplished.

Then there's Spiderman, ostensibly bitten by a radioactive spider that transferred to him enormous powers of agility, intuition, and speed. Nonetheless, he lives a lonely life unable to reveal his true identity and is treated as a nerd by fellow classmates (particularly the good-looking females). His innate goodness and self-deprecating humility is matched against the limitless megalomania of insanely brilliant villains hoping to rule the world. Remaining true to who you are despite overwhelming opposition, operating sacrificially without reward or recognition, and enduring the pain of being misunderstood are all values that speak to a male.

Then there's the Incredible Hulk, a mild-mannered scientist carrying a ferocious untamed beast within. Rage triggers the metamorphosis from skinny and retiring male to gigantic shirt-ripping, muscle-bound freak of nature. Reviled by society, he nonetheless battles forces of evil of epic proportions. Every man knows there is some beast within that must be harnessed lest it destroy him and others.

Are you starting to see the trend here?

Men, virtually all men, love to create and follow heroes. The core values that such superheroes embody draw men like magnets. (Lest you think comic books are only for children, look at the box-office-smashing sales figures for action-hero movies in the last ten years. It isn't only adolescent boys flocking to the theaters.)

Please Enter by the Side Door

What does this have to do with getting men to talk? A wife who can get her husband to talk about the man (or woman) he most admires (his hero) is going to have direct access to his core values. Yet, as a counselor friend says, "To gain such entry a wife will have to use the side door of his heart rather than the front door." Asking, "Who is the one person you admire most and why?" will allow him to safely begin discussing what character traits he most embraces. That will begin to explain his core value system.

Once you ask the question, you will likely hear about the sixth-grade baseball coach who gave him a chance to play, or the female high-school science teacher who entered his project into the state competition, or the pastor who spent time with him after his mother died. It may be the father who worked three jobs to put him through college. Or the uncle who patiently taught him to fly fish one summer and instilled his love of the outdoors. Regardless of the specifics, what you will hear is what he admires in other people.

Don't assume it's always other men that your husband may admire most. When we were serving a small rural congregation during our seminary days, Bob once hosted a Saturday morning breakfast for men (wives, note again the power of food to gather a male audience). Gathered around the table that morning were farmers, factory workers, county employees, and a few retirees. It definitely was not what you might call a group of "sensitive males." Most of the guys worked with their hands for a living, and their sunburned faces and weathered hands testified to that fact.

A guest professor from our seminary was the speaker that day. A wise, stately, and noble person, he opened the breakfast with a question that surprised even Bob. "Gentlemen, what do you remember about your mother?"

Bob wasn't sure that was the best discussion starter given the high octane, testosterone-based audience the professor was addressing. But what happened next was a moment he will never forget.

There was a long drawn-out silence (we referred to this earlier as "dead air") before the first man spoke. "My mother was one of the finest women who ever walked this earth…" The aging farmer went on to explain how, even though it was the Depression and they had little to wear, she ironed their shirts and made sure he and the rest of the family were in church each and every Sunday.

Another elderly gentleman said, "My mother used to take us to church every Sunday, and she gave us a quarter for the offering even when she didn't have a quarter…" With that he began to weep. Soon the entire table of men dissolved in a sea of tears as they all reminisced about their mothers long gone.

Now we know why the professor asked the question—he knew you can get men to talk about the person they admire most (and many men admire their mother for her sacrifices).

Men are motivated by their core values. If a wife asks her husband what person he admires most and why, she may be sitting there for the next two hours.

Question 3: "What's the best compliment anyone ever paid you?" (Topic: Need for Respect)

Now, even decades later, Bob becomes emotional when he tells this story.

Growing up, Bob loved the outdoors and all the typical sports boys enjoy, though he was never a natural athlete. Entering junior high, he was a scrawny kid who joined the debate team after he tried to play football and almost broke his neck on a blocking sled.

Worse yet, his gym teachers were all former military drill sergeants (we're not making this up). They, of course, delighted in the fine art of humiliation and ridicule as a tool of motivation. They quickly singled him out, along with other underweight kids, for particular mockery and derision (a method that may work well in boot camp but is a wrecking ball for the self-esteem of thirteen-year-old boys).

Each class was a new day in purgatory. Bob's ninth-grade gym teacher was transferred to his school from another junior high in the district for allegedly hitting a kid with a closed fist (this was before the days of litigation against teachers). Bob later watched him actually threaten a boy with a baseball bat.

By the sheer grace of God, Bob survived those ugly middle years—barely—and finally entered his sophomore year of high school. The summer before, he grew almost six inches. With his growth spurt came some athletic prowess, and he began to excel in gym-class soccer and volleyball, and even tried out for the tennis team. However, he discovered his real ability was in arguing (they call it debate), and by the end of his sophomore year he was competing on the varsity level with seniors. Yet, for all his progress, in his own mind he was still the short, scrawny kid who got picked on every day and humiliated by gym teachers back in junior high.

Then one day his gym teacher, who happened to be the high-school varsity football coach, asked all the boys to line up for uniform inspection. He walked up and down the line with a toothpick in his mouth and a sly grin on his face. The coach stopped when he got to Bob and pointed at him.

Oh great, Bob thought, *here it comes again.*

Then this coach said something that forever changed Bob's life.

"Moeller, I read about you in the school newspaper. You're in debate, aren't you?"

"Yes, sir," Bob answered, a slight catch in his voice.

"You're winning a lot of tournaments, aren't you?"

"Yes, we are."

He smiled. "Good for you. You keep up the good work. We need people who can think on their feet." He turned and addressed the rest of the class. "Not everybody here is going to be a great athlete. It really doesn't matter if you are or you aren't. What matters is that you find what you're good at and give it your best, like Moeller here. That's what life is all about, gentlemen."

Bob was stunned. It took a moment to absorb what had just happened. After years of seeing himself as the weak and picked-on failure, he was suddenly respected, even admired, by a gym teacher and coach. Bob's debate team won the state championship two years later.

That one compliment changed his life.

Mark Twain once said, "I can live for two months on one good compliment." The coach may never have realized it, but that day he made a friend for life in Bob.

A Complimentary View of Marriage

One of the strongest needs your husband has is for someone to believe in him and respect him. From the time he is a little boy to the time he reaches manhood, he is listening to hear if anyone believes he has what it takes. If you want to get your husband to talk, ask him about the best compliment anyone ever paid him.

Apparently the new bride in the white-hot sizzling book of wedded physical love, also known as the Song of Songs, understood her husband's need for respect and affirmation:

> My beloved is radiant and ruddy,
>> outstanding among ten thousand.
> His head is purest gold;
>> his hair is wavy
>> and black as a raven.
> His eyes are like doves
>> by the water streams,
> washed in milk,
>> mounted like jewels.
> His cheeks are like beds of spice
>> yielding perfume.
> His lips are like lilies
>> dripping with myrrh.
> His arms are rods of gold
>> set with topaz.
> His body is like polished ivory
>> decorated with lapis lazuli.
> His legs are pillars of marble
>> set on bases of pure gold.
> His appearance is like Lebanon,

choice as its cedars.
His mouth is sweetness itself;
   he is altogether lovely.
This is my beloved, this is my friend,
   daughters of Jerusalem.
                (Song of Songs 5:10-16)

(An aside to wives: Why not read to your husband from the Song of Songs? Affirm the great lover he is. It's a subject he'll want to talk about. Be prepared not to finish the book.)

Men can go a long time on one good compliment from their wives. In fact, they may go a lifetime on it.

Bob remembers meeting a Navy veteran who had served on a ship during World War II. He had a sign in the rear window of his car that said, "If you served on [my ship] please honk." Sensing his military service was an important part of his identity, Bob asked him to tell him more. It turns out this man served in the South Pacific and was assigned to the crow's nest to search for enemy ships or submarines that might be lurking nearby.

"One day I spotted something on the horizon," he said. "It was an enemy ship. I immediately alerted the bridge." The retired gentleman then seemed to stand taller and straighten his shoulders. He looked at Bob and said, "They told me I did good that day. Yup, they said I did good."

Circumvent the Seductress

Wives, never underestimate how much your husband needs your respect, admiration, and belief in him. How else do you think emotional affairs get started in the workplace? Is it with a seductive smile or a revealing wardrobe? Rarely is that the case. It usually begins with a female coworker affirming a man's work or performance, followed with respect-filled questions.

"How is it that you can get so much work done in such a short time?"

"Where did you learn to do what you do so well?"

"You're amazing—I hope the company appreciates what you bring to the table each day."

As your husband's spouse, why not say and do the things that will attract him to you? Why not circumvent the "seductress" by complimenting him and communicating your respect? Ask your husband questions that build him up, affirm his best strengths and gifts, and assure him of your unconditional respect. This will prove far more attractive to him than the skimpiest negligee, the deepest red lipstick, or the most alluring perfume (though none of these things will hurt the cause of your marriage either).

Question 4: "Growing up, who made you feel the most loved and why?" or "If you could spend just one more day with someone you've lost, who would that be?" (Topic: His Love Language)

Whenever we go out to our favorite family restaurant, our two youngest daughters can order Bob's meal for him without asking. "He'll have the honey-mustard chicken, a glass of skim milk, and for dessert a piece of pumpkin pie with ice cream," they'll tell the waiter.

It's not so much that he's a creature of habit, but the menu evokes some strong and precious memories for him—particularly the pumpkin pie. It seems his Swedish immigrant grandmother was a remarkable cook. Having settled on the windswept prairies of North Dakota just after the turn of the twentieth century, she and her husband raised seven children, the fifth of whom was Bob's mother, Inez. His parents often took him back to the farm during summer vacation and other holidays.

Bob would wake up in the old yellow farmhouse, clomp down the wooden stairs to the main floor, and be drawn to the kitchen by an aroma of fried eggs, bacon, homemade bread, and grape juice served in cut-crystal goblets. His grandmother, no more than five feet wearing heels, had soft, wavy black hair held up with bobby pins. She wore wire-rimmed glasses and an ornate homemade apron.

Each morning she greeted all her grandchildren in a combination of broken English and Swedish. "Uff da mia," she would say (the equivalent of "Oh my goodness"). "What would you like for breakfast?"

Around that wooden table, Bob and his siblings would eat and laugh and simply enjoy farm life with their elderly grandmother. At lunch she would usually produce a huge homemade pumpkin pie for dessert. "Ja, I made this because I know it is Bobby's favorite." It wasn't the thick brown crust, the nutmeg-spiced pumpkin custard, or the homemade whipped cream piled high that made it so special.

It was the fact it was served with unconditional love. Her act of service—making Bob his favorite pie—was his love language, and she spoke it fluently. The saddest day of his entire childhood was the day she died from cancer. The best friend he ever had was gone, never to return. That's one reason why, decades later, Bob still orders pumpkin pie.

Speak His Language and He'll Talk to You

Wives, do you know your husband's love language? According to Gary Chapman, the five love languages are words of affirmation, gifts, physical touch, quality time, or acts of service. Do you know who showed your husband the most love growing up and what they did to show it?

Why is that so important to know? Because it's precisely the information you need in order to make your husband feel loved all over again—and if he feels loved, he will talk to you.

Paul writes to Timothy, his young protégé in the ministry, and reminds him of those who loved him and passed on to him a godly heritage:

> I have been reminded of your sincere faith, which first lived in your grandmother Lois and in your mother Eunice and, I am persuaded, now lives in you also...
>
> But as for you, continue in what you have learned and have become convinced of, because you know those from whom you learned it, and how from infancy you have known the Holy Scriptures, which are able to make you wise for salvation through faith in Christ Jesus (2 Timothy 1:5; 3:14-15).

No doubt Timothy talked a great deal about the tremendous influence his mother and grandmother had on his spiritual life. They were likely his choice for the people who loved him the most growing up.

Wives can learn so much about their husband's heart and what moves it by asking questions such as, "Who was your best friend growing up and why?" "Who are the people that made you smile inside when you would think of them?" "Who really understood you?"

Who Does He Miss the Most?

Here's another question that holds tremendous power in a man's heart: "Who is the person from your childhood you wish you could spend one more day with?" As your husband responds, you will likely hear tenderness in his voice, see a nostalgic tear in his eyes, and catch a smile that tells you he is hyperlinking to a person who once loved him and is now gone. More than just a journey down memory lane, it may be the opening of an expressway to his heart that you have not traveled before. Even the most hardened and seemingly detached men can sometimes be reached this way.

There is a well-traveled story of a nun who worked with male inmates in a prison. She made an arrangement with a greeting card company for Mother's Day. They gave her enough cards that each prisoner could pick up one if he wished to do so. Expecting only a small response, she was amazed to see all the cards disappear within a few hours. Even in such a harsh and loveless setting, the memory of a loving mother still stirred a brief moment of tenderness in the inmates' hearts.

Let Him Walk You to the Door

Simply because a husband doesn't say much about love doesn't mean he has no interest or capacity to love. Rather, his feelings of love often lie buried just under the surface, sometimes concealed by years of hurt, rejection, disappointment, trauma, loss, and loneliness.

If you let your husband talk long enough, he will eventually walk you right to the door of his heart. And when he cracks open the door just an inch or two, a cascade of emotions can suddenly come flooding out.

If your husband is willing to open his heart even for just a moment and talk about who loved him the most and why, or who he misses the most, you can walk in before he closes it. If you are willing to positively respond to his display of deep feelings with love, sympathy, and support, he will likely no longer feel alone under the pile of long-buried grief and sadness. You can begin caring about his pain, and that will draw him to you. When he feels drawn to you, he will start talking to you.

Once Cheryl learned of the enormity of Bob's sense of loss over his grandmother's death, she began doing small things to tell him that she cared. She made pumpkin pie for dessert, helped him make big Saturday morning breakfasts for the children, and even bought him a gift certificate to a Swedish restaurant fifty miles away. She discovered, and rightly so, that one path to his heart was through recalling the memories of his precious grandmother.

One way a wife can discover the path to her husband's heart is to ask him the right questions, and then act on the information she learns. The rewards can be enormous and truly a life-changing event for their relationship.

Question 5: "What would you most like to be remembered for?" (Topic: Legacy)

On the back of a lonely gravestone in London, England, are engraved these remarkable words:

JOHN NEWTON, Clerk [preacher],
once an infidel and libertine,
a servant of slaves in Africa was,
by the rich mercy of our
LORD and SAVIOUR JESUS CHRIST,
preserved, restored, pardoned,
and appointed to preach the Faith he
had long laboured to destroy,
near 16 years as Curate of this parish,
And 28 years as Rector of St. Mary Woolnoth.

This is, of course, the epitaph of the famous hymn writer, John Newton. He is the author of one of the world's most well-known and well-loved hymns, "Amazing Grace." Newton wanted to be certain that grace would be his legacy. He wanted his life to testify to the grace that rescued him from the hellish decks of slave trading ships and transformed his life so amazingly that he eventually became chaplain to the Queen of England.

A Legacy of Right or Rot?

Men are concerned with the question, "What difference will my life have made once it's over?" As the years pass they begin to ask, "What will my children and grandchildren say about me?"

Pastor Charles Swindoll tells the story about a busy father who had to break the news to his wife and kids that he couldn't go on summer vacation with them. Things were just too stacked up at work. Instead, he helped his family pack their suitcases, map out the exact route they would take, and then bid them all good-bye. The children were naturally disappointed but said they understood.

Somewhere during the early part of the trip, the family passed by a man standing on the side of the road holding a sign. One of the kids shouted from the backseat, "Mom, did you see that guy? It looks like Dad." The mother thought he looked familiar too. She turned around and headed back to find the wayfarer. As the vehicle got closer, the kids screamed with delight. It was their dad!

"Why did you do that to us?" one of the children asked.

The father grinned as he threw his bags into the car. "Because someday I'm going to be dead and gone, and I want all you kids to remember that your dad was a fun guy."

The book of Proverbs addresses the importance of a man's legacy:

> The name of the righteous is used in blessings,
>   but the name of the wicked will rot.
>
> (Proverbs 10:7)

Most men and women want to be remembered in a positive light. Yet, for males, how they are remembered is particularly compelling. Men want to believe they made a difference. A wife can often get her husband to talk by asking the simple question, "What would you most like to be remembered for?"

While he may not be able to give an immediate answer or articulate it with clarity, it will start him thinking. It may take hours, days, or even weeks, but he will return to that topic sooner or later. "Remember when you were asking me what I'd like to be remembered for? Well, I've been giving that some thought..."

Why is it important to a wife's relationship with her husband that she understand the legacy he hopes to leave? It will enable her to understand what motivates him today. She will perhaps learn the reason behind many of his actions. Why does he get up early each morning to be the first person at work? Why does he volunteer so many hours at the church? Why is he so upset when someone accuses him of being dishonest? Why does he want his son or daughter to join him in the family business?

One way or another, all these questions will be answered if you begin to understand the meaning of legacy in a man's life.

A Soul Heir to the Estate

Just a year before Cheryl's father died, he expressed regret that he did not have a large estate to leave to his children and grandchildren. Yet, as a minister of the gospel, Roy had spent forty years of his life leading people to saving faith in Jesus Christ. Even in his final years his concern was for the souls of others. He would get out a phone book and call people from past churches who he knew were not Christians. He called to urge them to accept Christ as their Lord and Savior while there was still time.

While he did not leave his children and grandchildren certificates of deposit, gold coins, and real estate holdings, he left them something far more important—a legacy of caring for the eternal souls of men and women. Just one example of the impact of this legacy is our daughter

Melissa and her husband, Stephen, who live overseas and regularly share their faith with others.

Did he make the right investment? According to Jesus he did: "What good will it be for someone to gain the whole world, yet forfeit their soul? Or what can anyone give in exchange for their soul? For the Son of Man is going to come in his Father's glory with his angels, and then he will reward each person according to what they have done" (Matthew 16:26-27).

There are a variety of ways a wife can ask her husband about the legacy he wishes to leave: "What are you the most proud of in your life?" "What do you hope our children remember you for?" "What is your single greatest accomplishment?" (A former president of the United States was asked that question after he left office, and he offered this astute reply: "That the kids still come home to visit us.")

Don't assume you know what your husband desires for his legacy. The only way to know for sure is to ask and then...to listen.

Question 6: "If you could spend the rest of your life doing what you enjoy most, what would that be?" (Topic: Dreams and Aspirations)

One of the newer entries in our cultural lexicon is the term *bucket list*. It comes from the euphemism "kick the bucket," and is a list of the things a person hopes to do before they die.

Males think about their dreams and aspirations even at an early age. One husband, feeling trapped in his unchallenging life as a salesman, privately confessed to his wife, "One day I would like to build a place like Disneyland, but it would be a replica of the Holy Land instead." It was actually a great idea, and a place similar to that now exists in Orlando, Florida.

While a legacy is what a man would like to be remembered for, dreams and aspirations are those things he would like to realize before he dies—and they too are important for wives to understand about their husbands.

Our children laugh because they've heard their dad's dream so many times. "We know," they will say, feigning boredom. "Dad wants to own a cabin with cedar siding next to a north woods lake complete with white birch trees, a Finnish sauna on the beach, and a sixteen-foot aluminum fishing boat." Bob has other dreams, but owning a remote cabin is definitely in the mix.

Dreams—Handle with Extreme Care

Do you know what your husband's secret or unexpressed dreams are? If not, you have a wonderful opportunity to get him to talk by asking him questions. Because dreams are typically nonthreatening, it's one of those subjects you can get to without a great deal of conversational foreplay.

You can pose the question in numerous ways: "If you had all the money and time you needed, what would you do for a year?" "What is it that you watch others do that you wish you were doing?" "What were your dreams as a young boy?"

It is extremely important that you respond to his dreams and aspirations with great care and respect. The last thing you should do is to discourage him ("What? You've got to be kidding!"), act too incredulous ("What in the world?"), or worst of all, laugh ("That's the craziest thing I've ever heard!"). Any of those three responses and your husband may never, ever risk telling you something that is so personal and important to him again.

In the book of Genesis we meet Joseph, a young man with God-sized dreams. Unfortunately, Joseph made the mistake of sharing his dreams with his jealous and insecure brothers. The Bible tells us,

> Joseph had a dream, and when he told it to his brothers, they hated him all the more. He said to them, "Listen to this dream I had: We were binding sheaves of grain out in the field when suddenly my sheaf rose and stood upright, while your sheaves gathered around mine and bowed down to it."

His brothers said to him, "Do you intend to reign over us? Will you actually rule us?" And they hated him all the more because of his dream and what he had said (Genesis 37:5-8).

Joseph's brothers were not only annoyed with his dream, they were enraged by it. As a result, they stopped just short of murdering him, selling him instead into slavery. Then they heartlessly led their father to believe that Joseph had been mauled to death by an animal.

When a wife asks her husband about his bucket list and he begins to reveal his dreams, she needs to treat them with respect and honor. "That's amazing, what a wonderful thing to want to do in life." "I never knew that about you, but I am so honored that you would share that with me." Or perhaps best, "I'd like to be part of making that dream a reality in your life."

I Have a Dream...

Men are motivated by dreams, and sometimes dreams are the only thing that keeps them going. It's what raises men above a life of "quiet desperation" and propels them forward toward a great goal.

We read the story of a young Abraham Lincoln, then a lawyer in his midtwenties, who traveled with some friends to New Orleans, where for the first time he witnessed a slave market. There he saw human souls bought and sold as if they were livestock. He looked at his friends and said, "Someday I'm going to hit that thing—and I'm going to hit it hard." With that he turned away in disgust. His dream was not for his personal pleasure or ambition, but to see dignity restored to human beings who had been entirely deprived of it.

There is hardly a man alive who doesn't carry around in his heart unspoken and unrealized dreams. Many husbands are waiting for someone with the patience, interest, and wisdom to draw out those dreams.

If you can get your husband to share his dreams, you should be prepared for a long conversation. He has thought about this subject over a period of years, if not decades. With the passing of time, those dreams have taken on increasing detail and clarity.

Don't Take It Personally

A word of caution—the dreams he expresses may at first sound as if they don't include you. Please don't be upset by that or, worse yet, let it start an argument. Chances are he just assumes you are already in the picture and therefore he didn't feel the need to mention it.

Bob doesn't want to live all alone in a cabin in northern Minnesota or by the Michigan lakeshore. He just assumes Cheryl is going to join him in decorating the cabin with canoe paddles on the wall, making north woods chili for supper, and enjoying hot saunas together (and whatever romantic activity may follow).

In most cases men want their wives to join them in their dreams, and they just assume you will be on board for the ride. While that may or may not be the case for you, don't become alarmed, depressed, or angry if the first time he shares his dream with you, it's a little rough around the edges.

But what if your dream is the opposite of his? Instead of a remote north woods cabin, perhaps you dream of a gigantic house in one of the busiest cities in the nation. Instead of enjoying a quiet life of solitude, perhaps you are dreaming of family and friends constantly streaming through your doors. Granted, it will take some imagination, negotiation, and unselfishness to bring these two dreams together—but that's the stuff of marriage, isn't it?

Remember, dreams are so personal they become almost sacred to men. Therefore, treating them as such is all-important in getting a man to talk. If you can get your husband to share his dreams, he is well on the way toward sharing his heart with you. Isn't that what you've wanted all along?

Question 7: "Tell me about two or three of the best days of your life." (Topic: Serenity)

One of the more famous prayers of the twentieth century, made popular by the Alcoholics Anonymous movement, has been attributed to various authors and is usually referred to as "The Serenity Prayer":

God grant me the serenity
to accept the things I cannot change;
courage to change the things I can;
and wisdom to know the difference.
Living one day at a time;
enjoying one moment at a time;
accepting hardships as the pathway to peace;
taking, as He did, this sinful world
as it is, not as I would have it;
trusting that He will make all things right
if I surrender to His Will;
that I may be reasonably happy in this life
and supremely happy with Him
forever in the next. Amen.

Part of the success Alcoholics Anonymous has enjoyed in helping men (and women) find freedom from soul-destroying addictions has been to recognize the need men have for tranquility. Deep within the male soul is a need for a time and a place where all is well with the world. It is here, in the inner recess of the heart, that he longs to find peace and quiet, a place where there is no crushing weight of responsibilities, no turbulent waters of family conflict, and no dark night of mysterious suffering.

Give Peace a Chance

One day we sat with a dear friend who was going through a rough stretch of the road in his life. He was feeling worn out and uncertain if he could carry on. He surprised us by sharing a memory from childhood that kept resurfacing: "I'm twelve years old again and I'm swimming with my friends on a summer's day. We're in a river surrounded by high rocks. Afterward we're sitting on those rocks looking out over the countryside. Everything in the world is right."

Willard Harley, a renowned marriage counselor, explains that this basic male emotional need is a desire for *domestic tranquility* (*His Needs, Her Needs: Building an Affair-Proof Marriage*, Revell, 2001). Peace...

tranquility...serenity. These are among a man's basic needs. A wife can reach deep into her husband's heart and get him to talk by asking, "Apart from our first kiss, wedding day, and honeymoon, what were two or three of the best days of your life?" He will likely venture a partial answer to determine if you will treat his special memories with the same value and affection he does.

It is likely that he will take you back, as our friend did, to his childhood. Those days were carefree and life was much less confusing, tumultuous, and complicated. Some of the best days for Bob were riding tractors with his father on the Great Plains, spending part of winter break in a cabin with a wood-burning stove, and skiing high above the clouds in Switzerland.

As we've stressed already, the best response is just to listen when your husband starts talking on a heart level. There is a place to say things like, "Wow, that must have been really special," "I wish I could have shared such a wonderful day with you," or "What a wonderful picture of peace; I can see why you enjoyed it so."

Once you discover what once brought him tranquility, why not try to reproduce that again in his life? At the very least you can help create short moments of tranquility for him at home. Perhaps you can put on relaxing music and just sit next to him in silence and let his exhausted heart take a short rest.

Let Not His Heart Be Troubled

Jesus spoke to the innate need men have for serenity when he offered this comfort to his disciples: "Peace I leave with you; my peace I give you. I do not give to you as the world gives. Do not let your hearts be troubled and do not be afraid" (John 14:27). He is speaking to a need that many men feel—to experience peace that the world cannot take from them.

We believe Jesus is that peace men are looking for. He is the freedom from trouble and fear we so long to achieve. We can experience that unshakable peace as we place our faith in the finished work of the cross. Perhaps the reason we males innately long for peace and serenity is because it was lost it in the Garden of Eden. It was there, after Adam's rebellion, that God said,

> "Cursed is the ground because of you;
>> through painful toil you will eat food from it
>> all the days of your life.
> It will produce thorns and thistles for you,
>> and you will eat the plants of the field."
> (Genesis 3:17-18)

Pain...toil...thorns...thistles...these are daily realities husbands face in trying to earn a living. Our faith teaches us that the new earth is that ultimate place of peace:

> Then the angel showed me the river of the water of life, as clear as crystal, flowing from the throne of God and of the Lamb down the middle of the great street of the city. On each side of the river stood the tree of life, bearing twelve crops of fruit, yielding its fruit every month. And the leaves of the tree are for the healing of the nations. No longer will there be any curse (Revelation 22:1-3).

Instead of pain, there will be peace; instead of toil, rest; instead of thorns and thistles, a tree of life with leaves for the healing of the nations. Something inside the heart of a man longs for such a day and rejoices whenever he experiences even a taste of it for a few fleeting moments in this life.

Raising the Bar

Getting your husband to talk is not simply a matter of asking him questions—it is asking him the right questions in the right way. We believe certain topics hold interest for most men, and when a wife asks in a sincere, nonthreatening, and accepting manner the questions we have talked about in this chapter, she will get her husband to talk. His answers may or may not be what she expected, but they will likely be the truth.

One discouraged wife called to tell us her husband would rather spend the night at a bar with friends than go out on a date with her. We felt bad for her, but we suggested she try asking him some of the questions from this chapter. The fact that her husband frequently goes out to a bar to converse is almost proof-positive

- He has a longing for relationships.
- He is seeking out a place where he will be heard and accepted for who he is.
- He has something he wishes to say to someone.

What is true of that husband is likely true of most men. When they believe they cannot have those three needs or desires met with their spouse (usually because of the hurting emotional and relationship dynamics between them), chances are they will begin looking for a place where they will be fulfilled.

If a wife can provide for her husband's needs to be heard and understood, he will eventually quit going elsewhere and seek her out instead.

It's wrong to think most men aren't interested in relationships. They are, but those relationships need to be rooted in an attitude of respect, patient listening, and sincerity without criticism, contempt, or rejection. There is, of course, a time and a place to challenge your husband's thinking if it's clearly wrong or misguided. But to begin, you should focus on letting him say what's on his heart and affirming him for doing so. If you do, he will talk.

The Big Question: But What About Me?

We cannot end this chapter on important questions to ask your husband without answering an important question wives may be asking at this point: *If I do the listening and he does the talking, when do I get to tell him what's on my heart?*

This is probably the number one concern wives who hear our advice ask. It's possible to read this book and conclude that your need to talk as a wife should be put on the shelf indefinitely. That is not our belief. As a wife, your emotional, spiritual, and physical needs are just as important to God as your husband's needs. When it comes to our value in God's sight, men and women are equally precious to our heavenly Father. As the apostle Paul instructs us, "There is neither Jew nor Gentile, neither slave nor free, nor is there male and female, for you are all one in Christ Jesus" (Galatians 3:28).

However, if your husband does not talk to you and is unresponsive to your efforts to get him to talk, you will have to start with things the way they are rather than the way you wish them to be. You will have to make the difficult decision that, for a season, you are simply going to listen to your husband in order to draw him out and connect with his heart.

The most effective way we know to do this is to say little and let him express his ideas and feelings until he has truly exhausted them. This may take one day, one week, or even several months to accomplish.

What do you do in the meantime with your hurting heart and unmet needs for conversation while you listen to your husband's heart? We suggest you talk to another mature and godly woman. Let her listen to you for as long as you need to talk. The reason we don't recommend you find another man to talk to is self-evident: more than one affair was begun when a frustrated or lonely spouse started pouring out their heart to a sympathetic coworker or friend.

Seek Out a Godly Female Mentor

We believe it's particularly beneficial to seek out an older woman (someone one or two life stages ahead of where you are) who enjoys a stable and loving marriage. The Bible clearly endorses this kind of mentorship:

> Likewise, teach the older women to be reverent in the way they live, not to be slanderers or addicted to much wine, but to teach what is good. Then they can urge the younger women to love their husbands and children, to be self-controlled and pure, to be busy at home, to be kind, and to be subject to their husbands, so that no one will malign the word of God (Titus 2:3-5).

Finding such a person is not always easy, especially if you have isolated yourself in the midst of your difficult marriage. We don't recommend you go to a family member or relative as that typically adds unwanted dynamics to your situation. If you tell your sister or mother all your marital problems, they will naturally take your side. Out of loyalty and sympathy toward you, they may develop anger and resentment toward your husband.

So don't go looking for sympathy at any price. Rather, start by talking to your pastor or his wife about your need for a female mentor in the church. They may know of someone willing to fill the bill. There may even by a team of trained female volunteers willing to reach out to you.

Children Not Allowed

We also don't recommend using your children (even if they are grown) as a sounding board for your heart. Children simply aren't emotionally equipped to serve as counselors to their parents—it's a burden too great to bear. They will find themselves torn between the two of you, often having to choose loyalties children should never have to make. Sadly, we have talked to more than one wife who, growing up, was forced to become her mother's counselor as the result of an emotionally detached husband or one who had left the marriage.

The result is always nearly the same—the child becomes codependent with her mother. Then as an adult, she struggles to form a healthy and natural bond with her husband. Remember the song "Billy Boy"? The sad refrain suggests a codependent relationship: "She's a young thing and cannot leave her mother." Chances are the mom turned to the young daughter one too many times and ended up making her feel guilty for falling in love with young William. Now she doesn't have the emotional freedom or permission to leave and start a happy life of her own.

Find a Counselor Grounded in God's Word

Another good option is to find a gifted female Christian counselor you can meet with regularly. But be certain she believes the Scriptures are without error and the final authority in spiritual matters. We have met far too many people who went out with the best of intentions to find a "Christian" counselor, only to have that person give them advice completely at odds with God's principles for life and marriage. Beware of those who tell you, "Life is too short to spend it in an unsatisfying relationship, so get a divorce," or "Do what's ultimately best for you, even if it means leaving your husband and children," or "You've outgrown this marriage—time to move on."

We acknowledge that there are sometimes tragic and unyielding circumstances, such as unrepentant adultery, where Scripture allows for the end of a marriage. Yet, God's desire and our life commitment are to try and save even those apparently hopeless cases.

A Cyber Coincidence?

We wish we could introduce you to all the couples who once believed that divorce was their only option. Today they are enjoying their marriage and rejoicing that they stayed together. Because of the miracle of God softening their hearts toward each other, a new chapter was opened in their relationship.

We met a woman at one of our marriage conferences who had been divorced from her husband for several years. Eventually, they each decided to visit a dating website to find the next person of their dreams. The website does not reveal names initially, so they corresponded for a number of months with a person known only by a pseudonym. Their interest in the other person grew, and they eventually talked by phone.

They were both stunned. The person on the other end of the line was the ex-spouse. Following that experience, they came to us for a week of intensive pastoral care, and God worked in their hearts in a great way. We received this note from the woman not long after:

> Ben and I both wanted to write and tell you that we were remarried on March 7. Every day I wake up and just praise God for the miracle he has done in both of our lives. We've come full circle from the dark days of years ago. The renewal of our marriage has been unbelievable. God has

taken care of all the details, restoring not only our marriage, but each of us in the process...We both know we can take no credit for this miracle; God's hands are all over it.

If you need to seek out a Christian counselor, we urge you in the strongest possible terms to find one who will encourage you to "change relationships, not spouses." That is, rather than getting a new spouse, keep the one you have and transform your relationship so that it works for both of you.

The Day Will Arrive

If the ideas we recommend in this book succeed in getting your husband to talk to you, the day will come (we can't say just when) when he will say, "Dear, it seems I've been doing the talking for a long while. I'd like to hear what you have to say." For now, it's a step of faith to do more listening than talking.

Let's review some of the Scriptures we have examined so far in our journey toward getting your husband to talk to you:

> The purposes of a person's heart are deep waters,
>> but one who has insight draws them out.
>> (Proverbs 20:5)

> To answer before listening—
>> that is folly and shame.
>> (Proverbs 18:13)

> Even fools are thought wise if they keep silent,
>> and discerning if they hold their tongues.
>> (Proverbs 17:28)

> Sin is not ended by multiplying words,
>> but the prudent hold their tongues.
>> (Proverbs 10:19)

My dear brothers and sisters, take note of this: Everyone should be quick to listen, slow to speak and slow to become angry, because human anger does not produce the righteousness that God desires (James 1:19-20).

Let us add one more important passage from God's Word, commonly known as the Golden Rule: "So in everything, do to others what you would have them do to you, for this sums up the Law and the Prophets" (Matthew 7:12).

If you long for the day when your husband will sit and listen to the deepest needs of your heart, then do to him now what you would have him do to you later. Listen to him for as long as it takes. The day will likely come when he turns to you and says, "So what's on your heart?" It will have been worth the wait.

Questions to Consider

1. Do you believe that men tend to get more of their identity from their work than women do? What does Genesis 2:15 teach us about the origins of the importance of work in a man's life? Why does a husband enjoy talking about his core competencies? Have you ever asked your husband about his?

2. What can you learn from your husband by asking him about the people he admires? What does Hebrews 12:1-2 teach us about the importance of heroes and role models in a man's life? Do you know who your husband's heroes are?

3. Why is knowing what was the best compliment anyone ever paid your husband a vital piece of information? What does showing disrespect do to the heart of a man? What can we learn about the importance of wives showing honor from the story in 1 Samuel 15:1-38? Do you show your husband honor in how you listen to him?

4. Who made your husband feel most loved growing up? Why

would this help you understand his love language? Who made Isaac feel the most loved during a difficult time in his life, according to Genesis 24:67? What do you think Rebekah did to help fill that missing place in his heart?

5. Do you think the issue of legacy is important to your husband? What legacy did Joshua hope to leave in Joshua 24:15? Do you know what your husband hopes his legacy will be? In what ways are you supportive of that?

6. Do you agree dreams and aspiration are particularly important to a husband? What was the dream King David passed on to his son Solomon in 1 Kings 8:17-18? Do you encourage your husband to share his dreams with you? How do you react when he does?

7. Why is it men seek peace and serenity in their lives? What is the type of peace Jesus offers in John 14:25-27? What would your husband say brings him peace and serenity? How effective are you in creating an atmosphere of peace in your home?

Learning from the Master: How Jesus Got Men to Talk

"As they talked and discussed these things with each other,
Jesus himself came up and walked along with them...
He asked them, 'What are you discussing
together as you walk along?'"

LUKE 24:15-17

For Bob it was one of the most devastating days of his life.

He stood helplessly by as the graph on the hospital monitor flat-lined. He looked down and saw his mother's face—after she had spent seven days in a coma—change color. "She's gone," his youngest sister said quietly. "The angels have come for her."

He remembered the last time he had spoken to her just a week ear-lier. She was sitting up in her hospital bed following surgery. "Good-bye, Mom, I'll talk to you again," he said quietly as he kissed her on the forehead. He never did.

The day after her death, he boarded a plane headed back to Chi-cago—and stared out the window the entire time. Even the flight atten-dant's helpful question, "Can I get you a beverage?" barely distracted his attention. Someone he had known so well and loved so much was now gone, snatched from this life suddenly and without mercy.

Two Men Caught Up in Despair

That same feeling must have been on the hearts of the two men as they walked from Jerusalem to the little village of Emmaus. It was three days after the sudden death and shameful crucifixion of one of their dearest friends, Jesus of Nazareth. The Bible paints the truly extraordinary events of their conversation this way:

> Now that same day two of them were going to a village called Emmaus, about seven miles from Jerusalem. They were talking with each other about everything that had happened. As they talked and discussed these things with each other, *Jesus himself came up and walked along with them*; but they were kept from recognizing him.
>
> He asked them, "What are you discussing together as you walk along?"
>
> They stood still, their faces downcast. One of them, named Cleopas, asked him, "Are you the only one visiting Jerusalem who does not know the things that have happened there in these days?"
>
> "What things?" he asked.
>
> "About Jesus of Nazareth," they replied. "He was a prophet, powerful in word and deed before God and all the people. The chief priests and our rulers handed him over to be sentenced to death, and they crucified him; but we had hoped that he was the one who was going to redeem Israel. And what is more, it is the third day since all this took place" (Luke 24:13-21).

One can only imagine the state of emotional trauma and confusion the two men were experiencing. Less than seventy-two hours had passed since Jesus had been beaten beyond recognition, nailed to a wooden beam till the blood ran thick, and left to die a merciless death in the scorching Middle Eastern sun—and all that in front of a mocking crowd. The two men walked along trying to make sense of the senseless.

Seizing the Opportunity

Precisely at this moment Jesus approached them. The Scriptures say he came alongside them.

Jesus took the opportunity to give them an extended lesson from the Scriptures about the promised Messiah. His point was clear: the Scriptures had prophesied that these things must happen to the Christ. As Jesus finished his discourse, he acted as if he were going farther down the road. But he had gotten the men to talk with him, and they wanted to continue:

> As they approached the village to which they were going, Jesus continued on as if he were going farther. But they urged him strongly, "Stay with us, for it is nearly evening; the day is almost over." So he went in to stay with them.
>
> When he was at the table with them, he took bread, gave thanks, broke it and began to give it to them. Then their eyes were opened and they recognized him, and he disappeared from their sight. They asked each other, "Were not our hearts burning within us while he talked with us on the road and opened the Scriptures to us?" (Luke 24:28-32).

Wives often assume their husbands will not talk, particularly about difficult emotions such as sadness, grief, and loss. Husbands seem to send signals that they would rather be left alone to deal with their hurts. A wife learns to take the cue he wants to be alone, leaving him to himself to deal with his wounds until he is ready to rejoin the family.

Jesus, however, did not take that tack with the two men on the road to Emmaus. He did several things that got the men not only to talk, but then to listen, and finally to invite him into their inner circle.

How Jesus Got Men to Talk

Jesus was a master at getting men to talk. Wherever he went, whatever the setting, regardless of the event, Jesus succeeded in getting men to talk. In this chapter, we'll look at several principles Jesus used to get men to openly discuss some of the most important topics in their lives. These lessons from Jesus are transferable, enabling wives to learn from the Master of male conversation how to get their husbands to talk to them.

1. Jesus came alongside men.

Jesus didn't confront the two men on their way to Emmaus. Instead, he used a strategy that is very effective with most men—he simply came alongside and walked with them as they continued their journey. He engaged them in shoulder-to-shoulder communication.

Overall, men are much more comfortable conversing this way rather than face-to-face. Women typically enjoy intense, eye-to-eye, face-to-face dialogue. It's a sign they are taking the conversation seriously and are fully engaged. Such intensity can easily intimidate men. They prefer a far less intrusive form of conversation.

Men are more comfortable standing next to each other and starting a conversation in a more oblique fashion. Wives can take a cue from this. If you're looking for your husband to talk to you, perhaps you should stand next to him when he's working on a task in the basement or polishing his clubs in the garage.

Wives, if you're dreaming of sitting in a cozy coffee shop next to a crackling fire amidst fresh scents of roasting coffee from Indonesian jungles, seated face-to-face over a small wooden table made from recovered urban wood, lost in each other's gaze as you pour out your hearts one soulful topic after another—you may need to adjust your expectations. Let's just say that's not most men's idea of the perfect date.

You're more likely to get your husband to talk by sidling up to him at the counter of a fifties-style diner with stainless-steel stools and enjoying together their famous big juicy burgers cooked on an open grill. Or you'll have a better chance getting him to talk moving in a slow line outside a sports stadium. Or he may start talking as you work your way down the driveway he's sealing for the winter with asphalt.

The principle is simple—if you wish to get a man to talk, come alongside him, don't come at him.

That was Jesus's strategy on the road to Emmaus, and it worked. The men welcomed him as a fellow traveler on their journey toward the village. Looking down the road, they walked on and talked on and on the whole afternoon.

---

2. Jesus used activity to initiate conversations.

Don't miss the fact that the three men were walking as they were talking.

As we said in an earlier chapter, men talk as the result of an activity; women see talking as the activity itself. The good news is it really doesn't matter what the activity is. You can be walking, cycling, or making a gourmet supper together for friends, and he will talk. You can be raking leaves, cleaning the living room, or walking down the aisle of a supermarket looking for your favorite barbecue sauce, and he will talk.

Notice how many times in the New Testament Jesus initiated a conversation with a man while that man was doing something. He first approached Peter, James, and John while they were fishing. He came up to Matthew while he was conducting his tax-collection (shakedown) business. He even appeared to Saul (later Paul) while he was traveling to Damascus. While you might enjoy a heart-to-heart conversation over a dinner table, your best chance for getting your husband to talk may be in an aluminum boat casting a shoreline for bass.

If you want your husband to talk to you, engage him in some activity you both find enjoyable and watch what happens.

---

3. Jesus gave men freedom to continue or discontinue the conversation.

The Bible clearly says Jesus offered the men the opportunity to bring their conversation on the road to Emmaus to a close (Luke 24:28-29). This is important because men are often sensitive to being trapped in conversations. None of us like being cornered by an overbearing relative at Thanksgiving who shows you the scars from his neck surgery.

Men particularly feel uncomfortable being drawn into a conversation they can't get out of.

That's why an essential strategy in getting your husband to talk involves giving him a choice. He can choose to continue or discontinue the conversation—he is free to go or stay. If men sense they are not being compelled to continue a conversation and the exit door is clearly lit, they often will choose to continue.

Jesus gave the distinct impression he was moving on down the road. But because the conversation had been so interesting and powerful, "they urged him strongly, 'Stay with us, for it is nearly evening; the day is almost over.' So he went in to stay with them."

An All-Volunteer Conversation Works Better

When our son Brent applied to the U.S. Army's Officer Candidate School, he found he was on a six-month waiting list. This despite the fact our nation was at war. Part of the attraction of the military is that it is an all-volunteer force. No man or woman is compelled to join against their will or convictions. When an activity is voluntary rather than compulsory, it holds a greater attraction for those interested in it.

It's much the same when it comes to conversation. When men are given the freedom to talk or not to talk, the result is usually much better than when they are sat down, cornered, or told they will talk about a subject now.

Bob's father was not one to initiate conversations easily. Yet Cheryl, who is a skillful listener, would often sit next to him at family gatherings, and he would talk for what seemed like hours on end. Bob would look across the table and see his father grinning from ear to ear and using his hands to describe how a combine worked during wheat harvest in the 1940s.

Cheryl never demanded Bob's father talk to her, nor did she corner him. She just gave him the freedom to talk about things he knew and enjoyed. Her genuine interest gave him incentive to keep going, and he would talk without end.

Jesus gave the two men on the road the clear body language he was willing to free them from the conversation. "Not at all!" they said. "We've been enjoying this conversation so much, we'd like to continue. Come home and have supper with us and stay the night."

Funny thing about men—force them to do something and they'll often run for the exits. Give them the option to walk, and they often choose to stay.

Giving Atheists the Benefit of Their Doubts

We use a similar approach with men who claim to be atheists but who come to us for help with their marriage. We proceed with pastoral care for their marriage, but when we get to a critical moment, we will say, "We understand you don't believe there's a God. We respect your right to think that way. The last thing we want to do is offend you. So, though we do have some thoughts and ideas for how your marriage could be saved and reconciled, it would involve talking about God. So perhaps it's best we end things right here."

"Well, it wouldn't offend me to hear what you have to say," the man will typically respond.

"No, we're afraid it might. That's why it's probably best to call it a game right here. It would be impossible to go on without telling you about our faith. That could be troubling to you, and we promised we wouldn't do that."

"No, really, Pastor. I can handle you talking about God. Go ahead and say what you were going to say about how God could help our marriage. I won't be offended—seriously."

"Really? It's your choice."

"I know and I appreciate that. Now, what was it you were going to say?"

By giving the man an out, he has chosen to stay and listen—and is in fact intrigued by what we might have to say. An opening for spiritual matters has been created big enough to drive a Mack truck through. We do go on and present the truth of how God can bring forgiveness, healing, and new love to a marriage through the gospel of Jesus Christ. The man can't (won't) get mad at us because he insisted we speak our convictions. By giving him the choice to leave or stay, he felt respected, honored, and even in control of whatever conversation follows.

---

4. Jesus recognized the value of food for creating conversation with men.

While using food as a way to get men to talk might appear too unspiritual, consider how many times profound teaching and instruction occurred while Jesus was eating with others. The feeding of the five thousand, lunch with Zacchaeus the tax collector, the Last Supper, and the shore lunch with the disciples after the Resurrection all involved men and food.

God Calls Men to Feast

The Old Testament high and holy days were usually accompanied by great feasts, such as the Festival of Tabernacles, the Festival of Ingathering, and the Passover. The description in the book of Acts of the growth and ministry of the early church makes special note of the value of eating together: "Every day they continued to meet together in the temple courts. They broke bread in their homes and ate together with glad and sincere hearts, praising God and enjoying the favor of all the people. And the Lord added to their number daily those who were being saved" (Acts 2:46-47). Indeed, the Lord's Table is one of the ordinances Jesus left behind for his church to follow and enjoy.

When our youngest son, Andrew, was three years old, he attended an evening communion service with us. As the ushers passed the plate down our row, Andrew, who hadn't eaten supper yet and thought this was his snack, grabbed a handful of broken crackers and shoved them into his mouth. We were horrified, the ushers were incensed, and Andrew was satisfied. Perhaps in his innocence our son was closer than any of us in his understanding of the Lord's Table as it was intended to be a feast we are given to enjoy. And feast he did (at least it was a feast for a three-year-old).

The power of food to convey spiritual meaning is enormous and something that speaks to men in particular. Jesus understood that and made effective use of it.

Make Food and Men Will Arrive

We often jokingly (actually not so jokingly) tell single women interested in attracting a man that one of the most effective strategies involves just one word: *food*. "Make it and they will come," to paraphrase a line from *Field of Dreams*. We recognize both men and women enjoy a good meal. Yet, it's our observation that men particularly enjoy great food. We hold our Sunday evening Moeller Singles Group sessions at a hamburger place. We have been told by the singles that the women come for the men and the men come for the food. It works for everyone.

Like it or not, men are attracted to women who understand the power of food to create joy, fellowship, and relaxation. There is perhaps more truth contained in folk songs than we care to admit, such as this simple ditty we referred to earlier and that many of us learned in elementary school:

> Oh, where have you been, Billy Boy, Billy Boy?
> Oh, where have you been, Charming Billy?
> I have been to seek a wife.
> She's the idol of my life.
> She's a young thing and cannot leave her mother...
> Can she bake a cherry pie, Billy Boy, Billy Boy?
> Can she bake a cherry pie, Charming Billy?
> She can bake a cherry pie,
> Quick's a cat can wink her eye.
> She's a young thing and cannot leave her mother.

Notice what it takes to attract young William. While the fair maiden apparently has good looks, winsome manners, and a charming personality, that's not what wins the boy's heart. It's the fact she makes a mean cherry pie. Now if our William can just persuade her to leave her mother, he's set for life as far as he's concerned.

Food can prove to be a powerful magnet in getting your husband to talk. Setting his favorite meal in front of him, going out to a restaurant he really enjoys, or just plopping down next to him with a bowl of corn chips drizzled with cheese and chili is going to get his attention.

Food tends to relax men, lift their mood, help them forget the worries of the day, and it often opens them up to conversation.

---

5. Jesus spoke to men's hearts.

The story of the meal with the two men from Emmaus has an unexpected ending: "Then their eyes were opened and they recognized him, and he disappeared from their sight. They asked each other, 'Were not our hearts burning within us while he talked with us on the road and opened the Scriptures to us?'" (Luke 24:31-32).

Start with Simple Questions

Jesus spoke to the hearts of these men—the place where they give and receive love. As we said in an earlier chapter, to speak to a man's heart may require that you begin a conversation with less threatening and more innocuous questions. Note the first thing Jesus asked these two men when he came alongside them earlier in the day: "What are you discussing together as you walk along?" It's reminiscent of the way Philip the evangelist would later approach the Ethiopian official in the book of Acts: "Then Philip ran up to the chariot and heard the man reading Isaiah the prophet. 'Do you understand what you are reading?' Philip asked" (Acts 8:30).

We've already discussed the value of asking your husband good, nonthreatening questions to get him to talk. Yet, while it may be important to start out that way, most men are by no means superficial. They desire to talk about the things that are in their heart just as much as women do. It's just that it takes a different approach to get them to do so than it does for most women.

When Men Find Their Hearts

We have found consistently that one of the key turning points in the healing of a couple's marriage occurs when a man "finds his heart," to quote a good friend. That's the moment when a husband comes in touch with deep emotions he has often buried for years, if not decades.

We know he has found his heart again when his eyes well with tears and he begins to cry. The tests we give may indicate that he has shut down his feelings and become emotionally detached. But the moment he finds his heart, that all changes.

We dealt with one couple where the husband frequently gave orders to his wife and overwhelmed her with his demands. She was feeling increasingly suffocated by his assertiveness and lack of sympathy for her. She was even thinking about leaving the marriage so she could breathe again.

As we began discussing his life's experiences, it was clear he had been raised by a mother with a temperament similar to his. She seldom told him she loved him, she barked orders, and she refused to show any sympathy for his hurts or feelings.

We prayed together and urged him to tell Jesus what his domineering and insensitive mother had done to his heart. He started the prayer and suddenly burst into tears with a cry so loud it could be heard in another room. He wept convulsively as the pain he had carried for three decades suddenly came cascading out. His wife reached over and lovingly embraced him. From that moment, he was a changed man. Putting his wife first, caring for her needs, and encouraging her to unburden her heart with him became his first priority.

A wife can learn from the example of Jesus. He spoke to the hearts of men. In this case he had spent the day proving from the Law and the Prophets that the Son of God must suffer the things he did and then rise again. The Word of God, sharper than any two-edged sword, had pierced their hearts and caused their hearts to "burn."

Men are not offended when you speak to their heart—they are motivated by it. Jesus knew and understood and practiced this truth in his earthly ministry. He spoke to the heart of a notorious and lonely tax collector when he said, "Zacchaeus, come down immediately, I must stay at your house today" (Luke 19:5). He spoke to the heart of a bewildered and nervous teacher, Nicodemus, when he said, "For God so loved the world that he gave his one and only Son, that whoever believes in him shall not perish but have eternal life" (John 3:16). He spoke to the heart of a brash and impulsive disciple when he said, "And

I tell you that you are Peter, and on this rock I will build my church, and the gates of Hades will not overcome it" (Matthew 16:18).

Men Long to Be Understood

How can Jesus's ability to speak to the hearts of men help you as a wife in getting your husband to talk? Start by realizing that underneath your husband's exterior, even if it appears rough or insensitive or impenetrable, lies the heart of a man who longs to be understood, honored, and loved.

When Bob was in his forties and living in Chicago, an officer in his church complained frequently about the monthly electric bill. He usually looked upset about something, rarely smiled, and seemed to have barely concealed anger that could boil over at any moment. He would actually follow Bob into the sanctuary on Sunday mornings with the electric bill in hand, demanding to know if Bob was leaving the lights on in the church basement. He seemed intent on continually finding fault and making life as difficult as he could. Finally, Bob asked for a meeting with the man and another leader in the church to try to reconcile.

The meeting began with the man's litany of complaints over such things as the light bill, the typing mistakes in the bulletin, and a host of other relatively petty matters. Then, without warning or provocation, the man burst into tears and said, "My dad never had time for me."

Bob sat stunned. What in the world did his relationship with his father have to do with how many kilowatts the church had consumed that month? That's when it hit Bob. *He has been following me in order to get my attention. He has been badly hurting on the inside, and he's had no one to talk to about it. He's not mad at me—he just needs a friend.*

From that evening on, Bob and this parishioner became friends. There were no more arguments. No more complaints. No more Sunday morning interrogations. Bob had found this man's heart, and from that day onward a real friendship began. Even years after we left the church, this friend appeared at the funeral of one of our parents and offered his sincere condolences.

Talk as Jesus Talked to Men

A wife who desires to speak to her husband's heart must begin with the conviction that his heart is worth reaching. She must believe that if she finds his heart, it will draw the two of them closer than they have ever been. She must be convinced that there is a lifetime of feelings, both good and painful, that he longs to share with someone. She must have confidence that God's Word, when spoken with deep respect and conviction, can reach the inner recesses of his heart.

The model of Jesus on the road to Emmaus is one any wife who wishes to get her husband to talk should consider. He came alongside the men in their hour of pain, he asked good questions and listened respectfully to their concerns, he made their journey his journey, he went only as far as he was invited, he related to them as friends over a meal, and he left them to themselves to consider all he had said.

No wonder they call Jesus the Master.

In the next chapter we examine the spiritual steps you can take to have the right heart and mindset in getting your husband to talk. These are not the steps your husband needs to take (though we hope he will one day), but the preparatory steps you can take to be used by God in getting him to talk.

Questions to Consider

1. Do you think wives are more comfortable with face-to-face conversation and men more so with shoulder-to-shoulder communication? How did Philip approach the Ethiopian official to start a conversation in Acts 8:26-40? What are some settings in which you can literally "come alongside" your husband to talk?

2. Would you agree that men talk as the result of an activity while women tend to see talking as the activity itself? How have you seen this principle at work in your marriage? How did Paul use activity to form a bond with Priscilla and Aquila

in Acts 18:1-4? What activities could you and your husband do to encourage daily conversation?

3. How does giving a man freedom to continue or discontinue a conversation actually encourage him to keep talking? In Luke 24:28, do you think Jesus was pretending he was going to walk on or was he serious about it? Have you ever attempted to keep your husband in a conversation he wanted to leave? Overall, was that a good idea or a bad idea?

4. Why do you think food attracts men to conversation? Why did so many of the Old Testament high and holy days involve feasting? How can meals be used to pass on spiritual lessons to the next generation, as in Exodus 12:1-28? How could you use food more often in your marriage to create opportunities for conversation?

5. Jesus seemed to be able to reach men's hearts. How did he do that? How can you tell if you're reaching your husband's heart? What was the sign that both Hezekiah and Peter had come in touch with their heart (see Isaiah 38:3 and Matthew 26:75)? Does your husband feel comfortable laying his heart's secrets open with you?

5

Change My Heart, O Lord

"I will give you a new heart and put a new spirit in you; I will remove from you your heart of stone and give you a heart of flesh."

EZEKIEL 36:26

One approach we use with hurting couples is to take them through five days of intensive pastoral care for their marriage (three hours a day for five days). Using the Word of God and prayer, our goal is to see them soften their hearts toward one another, thus creating a new and deeper level of spiritual and emotional intimacy. One of the most common statements we hear at the end of our week is this: "I came here thinking it was my spouse who needed to change. I was hoping and praying that you were going to fix them. Now, after all these days, I've realized it was my heart that God needed to change."

That statement is one of the surest signs God has been at work in the person's life. Regardless of the myriad problems our spouse may have, there is always room for the Lord Jesus to make needed changes in our own lives.

While we have looked at a number of practical techniques and strategies for getting your husband to talk, there are steps you need to take to make this effort successful. Yes, it begins with you (though we hope it will not end with you). You will need to consider changing your relationship with God before asking him to change your husband's relationship with you.

Step One: Confirm my relationship with Christ.

One of the assumptions of this book is that the majority of wives reading it are already trusting in Christ alone for their salvation. Yet, that assumption may not be true in your case. Perhaps you consider yourself a Christian, but allow us to ask two questions the late D. James Kennedy would ask people:

Question 1: If you were to die tonight, do you know with certainty you would go to heaven?

Before you answer that question too quickly, consider his second question.

Question 2: If you were to die tonight and stand before God, and he were to say to you, "Why should I let you into my heaven?" what would you say?

Perhaps your answer to the second question is something like, "I'm a good and moral person," or "I've never done anything really wrong, like committing a serious crime," or "I'm a member of a church and I was baptized, confirmed…" or, "God is love, so he must let everyone into heaven. He could never send anyone to hell."

You May be Sincere, Yet Sincerely Wrong

Unfortunately, none of these answers or assumptions will admit you to heaven. They are based on your own efforts and all fall short of God's standard of perfection. The Bible starts with some bad news for all of us: "for all have sinned and fall short of the glory of God" (Romans 3:23).

Yet, the literal meaning of the word *gospel* is "good news." So where is the good news for us if we have all sinned and deserve to be locked out of the gates of heaven? It's found in the message of grace: "For it is by grace you have been saved, through faith—and this is not from yourselves, it is the gift of God—not by works, so that no one can boast" (Ephesians 2:8-9).

What is this grace that saves us? It is the unearned favor or mercy of God that allows him to cancel our sin and guilt. "But where sin increased, grace increased all the more, so that, just as sin reigned in death, so also grace might reign through righteousness to bring eternal life through Jesus Christ our Lord" (Romans 5:20-21).

Heaven is a free gift—not one that can be earned or deserved by our good works, membership in a church, or good intentions.

How do we obtain such a free gift? We place our trust in the death of Christ upon the cross for our sins:

> We all, like sheep, have gone astray,
>> each of us has turned to our own way;
> and the LORD has laid on him
>> the iniquity of us all.
>> (Isaiah 53:6)

The Power of the Cross

It was on the cross that Christ paid the full penalty for our sins and canceled our debt forever: "For God was pleased to have all his fullness dwell in [Christ], and through him to reconcile to himself all things, whether things on earth or things in heaven, by making peace through his blood, shed on the cross" (Colossians 1:19-20).

The question is: Have you placed your faith in Christ alone for the gift of eternal life?

If not, this would be the time to do so. If you wish to see the love, grace, and power of God at work in your husband's life, you need first to be in right relationship with God yourself.

Faith and Your Favorite Living Room Chair

What is faith? Faith is not just knowing the truth of the gospel nor simply agreeing with it. Even the devil knows the gospel message and agrees it is true, but he will never be in heaven. Instead, you must take the vital step of trusting in Christ.

What does it mean to trust? If I asked you if your favorite chair in your living room would hold you up, and you answered yes, that by itself would not show trust in the chair. Only if I asked you to sit in that chair and you did, only then could you say that you have true trust or faith in that chair. It's similar with receiving eternal life. You can say you know Jesus, you can say you agree with Jesus, but not until you put your entire trust in him and begin to follow him can you say you have saving faith in him. As the Bible promises us, "For God so loved the world that he gave his one and only Son, that whoever believes in him shall not perish but have eternal life" (John 3:16).

Are you ready to take that step of faith? If so, here is a prayer to help you:

> *Lord Jesus, I thank you that you loved me so much you came to this earth to die on my behalf. I believe you are the Son of God, that you lived a perfect life, and that you offered your life as a full payment for my sins. I ask your forgiveness for all I have done wrong, and I place my faith in you and your death on the cross and resurrection. I receive now by faith the gift of eternal life. Thank you that heaven is mine as a free gift. Thank you that I have become your child—now and forevermore. Amen.*

The Answer That Will Open Heaven's Gates

Now, if you were to die tonight and God were to ask you, "Why should I let you into my heaven?" what would you say? If your answer is, "Because I am trusting in the finished work of Christ on the cross, and I believe he died and rose again for the forgiveness of my sins," the doors will open wide. God Himself will welcome you and say, "Well done, good and faithful servant!...Come and share your master's happiness!" (Matthew 25:23).

There is no more important step if you wish for God to change your husband's heart than to ask him to change your own first. Trusting Jesus Christ as your Lord and Savior is the starting point. What can God accomplish through a wife who is a believer? Listen to this promise from Scripture: "Now to him who is able to do immeasurably more than all we ask or imagine, according to his power that is at work within us, to him be glory in the church and in Christ Jesus throughout all generations, forever and ever! Amen" (Ephesians 3:20-21).

Now that you have confirmed your relationship with Christ, it's time to move on to the next step.

Step Two: Do a searching spiritual inventory.

One day we were approached by a wife who was distressed about her husband. They had married young, and the intervening years had not gone well. According to her, he was weak, submissive, and lacked assertiveness. But her main complaint was, "He never talks to me." She went on (for almost thirty minutes) to express dismay that her husband was still under the domination of a controlling mother—one who never let him or anyone else get a word in edgewise.

The longer we listened, the more we began to suspect this husband had married the emotional replica of his overly talkative and domineering mother. When we finally were able to speak, we lovingly suggested to the wife that if she wanted to get her husband to talk to her, she may need to make changes in her own life first. If she hoped to see her husband open up and become expressive, she would need to do a searching spiritual inventory of her own attitudes and behaviors.

Spotting Fault Lines

Jesus has a hard word, but a good word, for all of us who are prone to see the faults of others more clearly than our own:

> "Why do you look at the speck of sawdust in your brother's eye and pay no attention to the plank in your own eye? How can you say to your brother, 'Let me take the speck out of your eye,' when all the time there is a plank in your own eye? You hypocrite, first take the plank out of your own eye, and then you will see clearly to remove the speck from your brother's eye" (Matthew 7:3-5).

That's why, to be spiritually prepared for God to work in your husband's life, you need to pray as the psalmist David prayed:

> Search me, God, and know my heart;
>> test me and know my anxious thoughts.
> See if there is any offensive way in me,
>> and lead me in the way everlasting.
>> (Psalm 139:23-24)

Could I Be Part of His Problem?

What do we mean by a searching spiritual inventory? We need to ask God to examine our lives and to help us answer the question, "Are there attitudes or actions in my life that keep my husband from talking to me?"

This is admittedly not a comfortable thing for anyone to do. Yet, in our experience, attitudes, behaviors, and responses (some unrecognized) on the part of the wife often contribute to her husband shutting down and not talking. These are primarily emotional and spiritual traits that step on the husband's damaged heart issues, most of which were in place before they got married.

Time for a Heart Exam?

As a wife, it's vital to examine your life and heart and be ruthlessly honest in your self-evaluation. This may be a place to ask a trusted friend, who has only your best interests in mind, to come alongside you and help you do an honest self-evaluation. (For help with this process, consider using our Personal Heart Exam, which is available in the appendix of this book or free online at www.forkeepsministries.com/heart_exam_13.html.)

This personal inventory will help you identify the various types of damaged hearts, as well as the sins of the heart that Jesus listed, that may be factors in your marriage. There are also sample prayers that can be a starting point for dealing with the spiritual and emotional dimensions of your damaged heart.

For a deeper discussion of this issue, you may wish to go online to purchase an e-edition of our book, *The Marriage Miracle: How Soft Hearts Can Make a Couple Strong*, which further explains the steps to healing your heart damage.

Six Questions that Could Change Your Marriage

Where do you begin taking such a spiritual inventory of your life? Here is a list of questions to ask yourself regarding your attitudes and behaviors toward your husband:

1.

Have I been overly verbal with my spouse?

We once took a six-hour road trip with a college friend who talked the entire six hours. We prayed for a flat tire or something just to be able to get out of the car.

If you are a talkative (perhaps a very talkative) person, that may just be the way you were born. On some personality tests, you will likely be rated as an extrovert or an expressive-responsive person. For the most part, it's a wonderful gift to have and to use for God's glory as you use words to establish and build meaningful relationships.

However, if you are married to a husband who is quieter and more introverted by nature, you may be burying him under an avalanche of your words and ideas. His heart is being damaged by the pressure you put on by doing all the talking and rarely allowing him to say a word. You are, in that case, "overly expressive." Listen to the various Scriptures that warn us about saying too much and listening too little:

> Sin is not ended by multiplying words,
>> but the prudent hold their tongues.
> (Proverbs 10:19)

> My dear brothers and sisters, take note of this: Everyone should be quick to listen, slow to speak and slow to become

angry, because human anger does not produce the righteousness that God desires. Therefore, get rid of all moral filth and the evil that is so prevalent and humbly accept the word planted in you, which can save you (James 1:19-21).

> To answer before listening—
> that is folly and shame.
> (Proverbs 18:13)

Unfortunately, a person can become so accustomed to doing all the talking that he or she assumes everyone is enjoying it. That may not be the case.

Pardon the Interruption

We were at a marriage weekend where a husband and wife were giving their testimony to God's restoring grace in their marriage. The husband, normally a reserved and quiet person, began to tell their story with joy and enthusiasm. Approximately two minutes into his description of their journey, his wife jumped in and began telling her side of the story. You could literally see his face fall. "I guess it's your turn," he said quietly and sat down. Everyone in the room felt bad for the husband. It was clear he wanted to tell his story, but his wife was accustomed to talking for both of them.

If you are a frustrated and disappointed wife, hurting and confused that your husband doesn't talk to you, you may wish to ask God, "Am I talking too much and listening too little to my husband?"

If you have been overly verbal in your marriage, then perhaps you need to confess the sin of self-focus. Ask God to give you an unselfish and sensitive heart toward others, particularly your husband, and allow you to be more interested in what he or others have to say than in what you have to say. The Bible challenges us, "Do nothing out of selfish ambition or vain conceit. Rather, in humility value others above yourselves, not looking to your own interests but each of you to the interests of the others" (Philippians 2:3-4).

Looking to the interests of your husband may mean you deliberately scale back your talking and give your spouse the chance to express his heart.

2.

Have I been overly dominant with my husband?

Some people are born more assertive than others, which partially explains why there are leaders and followers in the world. These two groups tend to be divided along the lines of bosses and employees in the workplace or generals and privates in the armed forces.

A more assertive personality is not necessarily a detriment to a marriage. However, if your assertiveness has progressed to dominance or even aggressiveness, that is a problem. This leads to imposing your thoughts and ideas and decisions on your husband without any true regard for his feelings or thoughts. It could be that your hyper-forcefulness or argumentativeness is further damaging his heart and shutting him down. That's why he doesn't talk to you.

The Scriptures speak of the difficulty of living with a contentious wife:

> Better to live on a corner of the roof
> than share a house with a quarrelsome wife.
> (Proverbs 21:9; 25:24)

> Better to live in a desert
> than with a quarrelsome and nagging wife.
> (Proverbs 21:19)

> A quarrelsome wife is like the dripping
> of a leaky roof in a rainstorm;
> restraining her is like restraining the wind
> or grasping oil with the hand.
> (Proverbs 27:15-16)

When an overly dominant wife is matched with an overly submissive husband, the result will be frustration and disharmony in the marriage.

Are you overly confident, assertive, or competitive with your husband? Does your assertiveness morph into aggressiveness? Do you always have the last word? Do you feel a tingle of satisfaction when he gives in and lets you have your way? Do you frequently interrupt or challenge him when he is trying to say something? Is he always the one to apologize first in an argument? Have friends complained that you are running his life? (We know that's not always a fair assessment, but often there is an element of truth in the criticisms we receive.) Is your husband showing signs of simmering anger, such as sarcasm, passive-aggressive behavior, and even occasional outbursts?

Submitting for Your Consideration

If the answer is yes to one or more of these questions, it may be time to pause and do some honest self-examination. Ask the Lord to show you if your self-confidence and assertiveness has crossed the line into controlling and dominating behavior. It may be time for you to practice a more submissive attitude in your marriage. Paul speaks to this principle in marriage:

> Submit to one another out of reverence for Christ.
> Wives, submit yourselves to your own husbands as you do to the Lord. For the husband is the head of the wife as Christ is the head of the church, his body, of which he is the Savior. Now as the church submits to Christ, so also wives should submit to their husbands in everything (Ephesians 5:21-24).

This is not the place for a detailed discussion about the meaning and application of *submission* as it is used in the Scriptures. Simply summarized, it does not mean blind obedience or servile acquiescence to whatever a husband might say. Rather, it is to voluntarily yield in love and honor to his spiritual leadership in the relationship.

One husband told us, "I feel walked on every day of my life." If that's the case, his wife is failing to practice biblical submission. She is likely allowing her emotional pain and spiritual pride to impose her will on him to protect herself from being hurt. As she sees it, her best defense is a good offense.

A Doorway, Not a Doormat

What does healthy emotional and spiritual submission look like in a marriage? A wife should pray for God to reveal to her the power and wisdom of biblical submission and then practice it. Submission is not becoming a doormat or losing a sense of individual personhood; it is a doorway to trusting God to work in your husband's life as you show him honor and respect. The apostle Peter highlights this in his instruction on marriage:

> Wives, in the same way submit yourselves to your own husbands so that, if any of them do not believe the word, they may be won over without words by the behavior of their wives, when they see the purity and reverence of your lives…[Your beauty] should be that of your inner self, the unfading beauty of a gentle and quiet spirit, which is of great worth in God's sight. For this is the way the holy women of the past who put their hope in God used to adorn themselves. They submitted themselves to their own husbands, like Sarah, who obeyed Abraham and called him her lord. You are her daughters if you do what is right and do not give way to fear (1 Peter 3:1,2,4-6).

An Atmospheric Change

Chances are you helped establish a pleasant atmosphere in your courtship or dating days. Your actions and reactions to your then boyfriend were for the most part calm, kind, loving, and easy to get along with. He felt free to talk to you. That's what helped lead eventually to your marriage.

This short paragraph from 1 Peter teaches some abiding principles that a wife can use (or return to) in creating the atmosphere and opportunity for her husband to talk.

First, she should honor her husband. That means treating his thoughts and ideas and desires with respect.

Second, it teaches she should display a gentle and quiet (undisturbed) spirit. Such genuine inner tranquility will be attractive to her husband.

Third, it says that she should put her trust in God rather than in her husband. A woman can take the risk of voluntarily yielding in love and honoring her husband because God has pledged to take care of her— even if her husband is less than sensitive or loving.

Finally, it says she should not live in fear. Fear is usually what motivates aggressive and controlling behavior. The controlling person thinks, *If I don't control everyone and everything around me, then something bad is going to happen to me.*

We believe a wife who honors her husband, displays a gentle and undisturbed spirit, puts her full trust in God, and refuses to live in fear is ultimately going to make it easier for her husband to talk. He will respond to each of her positive spiritual characteristics in a positive way. She will have gotten her husband to talk without resorting to aggression, coercion, or manipulation.

Ask Noncontrolling Questions

What are some things you might say to your husband to back away from dominance or control?

- "Is this what *you* really want to do or is this just what you think *I* want to do?"
- "If you could really say what you're thinking, what would you say?"
- "What if we spent an entire day doing what you enjoy most?"

Statements like these convey the truth that your husband does not need to comply with your every wish or whim. Rather, he has the complete freedom to say what he longs to say and to do what he longs to do. When he no longer feels controlled, he is likely to feel closer to you, and when he feels closer, he will start talking.

3.

Do I believe I am in some fashion superior to my husband?

"Well, of course not," you might answer. "How could you suggest such a thing? Who do you think I am—some type of egomaniac?"

No, we don't assume or think you're an egomaniac (at least no more than the rest of us). But do you ever find yourself dwelling on his faults, blind spots, and habits that truly irritate you? Do you ever find yourself thinking, *Why can't he be more like me?*

Pride, the Great Pretender

One of the most dangerous elements of pride is its ability to disguise itself. Rarely does the sin of pride march up to the front door of our life, ring the bell, and say, "Hi, I'm the sin of Pride, and I'm here to take over your life and ruin your marriage. Just open the door and let me walk in, and I'll make a mess of your marriage in no time flat."

No, our adversary is much too clever to approach us in that way. Rather, pride usually works its way into our marriage by attaching itself like a parasite to some legitimate need or desire we have. It does so by pretending to be other than what it is.

For example, we often explain to couples that much of the heart damage in their lives can be traced back to their home environment. We have had wives stop us right there with comments such as this. "You know, Bob, I think that's really true of my husband's family. There are a lot of problems on his side. Fortunately, I grew up in a loving and stable family. I can't think of anything my parents might have done wrong."

Such a person is utterly sincere. They truly believe they grew up in the perfect (or near perfect) home. They truly can't think of anything that might have happened to damage their heart. How does such a claim of the perfect home square with Scripture?

> Who can say, "I have kept my heart pure;
> I am clean and without sin"?
> (Proverbs 20:9)

> We all, like sheep, have gone astray,
> each of us has turned to our own way;
> and the LORD has laid on him
> the iniquity of us all.
> (Isaiah 53:6)

> God looks down from heaven
> on all mankind
> to see if there are any who understand,
> any who seek God.
> Everyone has turned away, all have become corrupt;
> there is no one who does good,
> not even one.
> (Psalm 53:2-3)

> For all have sinned and fall short of the glory of God
> (Romans 3:23).

We hope the point is obvious: all of us—all homes—struggle with sin and its impact on our lives. If there were any perfect people, parents, or families, the atoning death of Christ would have been unnecessary (at least for them). We recognize that on the continuum of healthy to unhealthy, some families fall on one end, some the other, and others in between. There certainly are better parents and worse parents as well as emotionally stable relationships and unstable relationships.

Don't Get Edgy

Yet every family and set of parents has fallen short of the glory of God. Sadly, the sin that impacts one generation is often passed on to the next. A proverb apparently quoted frequently in ancient Israel goes this way:

> The parents have eaten sour grapes,
> and the children's teeth are set on edge.
> (Jeremiah 31:29; Ezekiel 18:2)

Why are we stressing the need to acknowledge our family's shortcomings? What does that have to do with getting your husband to talk?

Because we are fallen human beings who have inherited a sin nature, pride has seeped into all our lives and families. That may lead us to believe our family is better than our spouse's family. As one woman told us, "The problems are all on his side of the family." There are no perfect parents, no perfect families, and no spouse who does not struggle with the impact of the sinful nature we all inherited from Adam. That's why it's important to do a searching spiritual inventory to determine if you feel superior to your spouse in some way. That subtle attitude of pride will come seeping through into your relationship, and your husband will sense it. If he receives the message that you think you are superior to him, he will shut down and not talk to you.

Do You Believe You Could Have Married Better?

How can we test our own hearts to see if we harbor thoughts of superiority or elevated status compared to our husband? Do you ever entertain thoughts such as these?

- "I married beneath me."
- "If I had life to do over again, I would choose a different spouse."
- "If he would just listen to me, he could be so much more."
- "If only I could change him."

What do all these statements have in common? The sin of self-focused pride.

How do we begin to combat such a danger in our soul? One practical way is to ask yourself, *If I had been raised in my husband's home and experienced the same difficulties he did, would I have handled life as well as he has? Would I have turned out just as good, or better, or perhaps worse?*

The truth is, if you had been raised in his circumstances you don't know how you would have turned out, so it's best not to judge him. The Bible tells us, "There is only one Lawgiver and Judge, the one who is able to save and destroy. But you—who are you to judge your neighbor?" (James 4:12).

A Heartfelt Confession

If you are given to judging your spouse, or feeling in some way superior, it's time to pray a prayer of confession:

> *Lord Jesus, I need to ask your forgiveness for comparing my husband to myself and concluding I'm better than he is. He has sensed my condescending attitude toward him—and it has damaged his heart. Lord, give me a spirit of humility toward him, remembering that I have not walked in his shoes nor lived his life.*
>
> *If I had done so, I might have fallen short of who he is today. Let me instead give you thanks that he would choose to live his life with me—unworthy as I am. Fill my heart with gratitude that I am his wife and that you brought me to him. Let me focus on his strengths rather than his weaknesses. As of today, let me forsake judging him and choose to give you praise for him instead. Amen.*

If that prayer seems too difficult or unnecessary, remember the parable Jesus told of two individuals who went up to the temple to pray:

> To some who were confident of their own righteousness and *looked down on everybody else*, Jesus told this parable: "Two men went up to the temple to pray, one a Pharisee

and the other a tax collector. The Pharisee stood by himself and prayed: 'God, I thank you that I am not like other people—robbers, evildoers, adulterers—or even like this tax collector. I fast twice a week and give a tenth of all I get.'

"But the tax collector stood at a distance. He would not even look up to heaven, but beat his breast and said, 'God, have mercy on me, a sinner.'

"I tell you that this man, rather than the other, went home justified before God. For all those who exalt themselves will be humbled, and those who humble themselves will be exalted" (Luke 18:9-14).

There is only one remedy for pride and that is humility. With humility comes the healing of relationships, and with the healing of relationships comes emotional intimacy, and with emotional intimacy comes talking to one another.

4.

Have I been feeling sorry for myself because he doesn't talk to me?

We just finished a discussion of what one author calls "obvious pride," that is, the idea that we are in some way superior to our spouse.

There is a second kind of pride that is just as prevalent but far less easy to detect. It's what that same author calls "hidden pride." What is hidden pride? It is self-pity that causes us to self-focus on our pain and misery.

"But wait," you might argue, "why shouldn't I feel sorry for myself? I have a husband who is aloof, emotionally detached, and never talks to me. What's wrong with being upset over a lonely marriage with little or no hope of things ever changing? Isn't that just facing my sad reality?"

Sinking in the Quicksand of Self-Pity

There's nothing wrong with acknowledging that you face difficult problems in your marriage. There's no wrong in admitting your current relationship (or lack of one) is causing emotional and spiritual pain. The problem occurs when you allow that pain to take center stage in your life. When all your time and energy goes toward feeling sorry for yourself, you have little left over to give to others. Self-focus easily morphs into self-centeredness, and self-centeredness is pride, and pride is a sin.

Besides the spiritual cost, there is an emotional price to pay for self-pity. It typically leads to despondency, despair, and ultimately depression. The more we feel sorry for ourselves, the less we can see of what God is doing (or wishes to do) in our lives.

That's the backdrop for an amazing story found in the gospel of John. It begins when Jesus comes across a man who has been paralyzed for thirty-eight years—perhaps his entire life. What happens next is a most unexpected dialogue between the disabled man and Jesus:

> Now there is in Jerusalem near the Sheep Gate a pool, which in Aramaic is called Bethesda and which is surrounded by five covered colonnades. Here a great number of disabled people used to lie—the blind, the lame, the paralyzed. One who was there had been an invalid for thirty-eight years. When Jesus saw him lying there and learned that he had been in this condition for a long time, he asked him, "Do you want to get well?"
>
> "Sir," the invalid replied, "I have no one to help me into the pool when the water is stirred. While I am trying to get in, someone else goes down ahead of me."
>
> Then Jesus said to him, "Get up! Pick up your mat and walk." At once the man was cured; he picked up his mat and walked (John 5:2-9).

An Identity Crisis

What does this story have to do with getting your husband to talk? If your husband is distant and detached, you may have experienced emotionally paralyzing pain for years or decades. You may have surrounded yourself with other women who are hurting in the same way.

As the years have gone by, the hope of healing in your relationship has all but faded away.

The discouragement from your marriage no longer merely impacts your identity—it is your identity.

If that's your situation, God's question to you may be, "Do you want to get well?" What might he mean by that? If God tells you to do something, are you willing to do it, or are you so invested in your pain and misery that you plan to spend the rest of your days feeling sorry for yourself?

In the biblical story the man never directly answers Jesus's question; instead, he begins a litany of excuses why he remains stuck where he is. His real disability is not his physical paralysis but a spiritual paralysis brought on by years of self-pity.

There is more than a little irony in this story. According to the legend of the day, angels would periodically come down and stir up the pool of Bethesda. It was believed the first person into the water would be healed. The paralyzed man lamented that he had never made it to the pool first—others always splashed in ahead of him. Yet, standing in front of him was Jesus, one far greater than the angels (see Hebrews 1:4).

Unfortunately, when we begin to feel sorry for ourselves, we end up missing the opportunities standing right in front of us. Instead, we rehearse over and over our list of excuses and rationalizations why things will never change or improve in our marriage. We watch in envy as others seem to find help, but we are left in our hopeless state.

A Checklist of Despair

Are you struggling with the sin of self-pity? Has discouragement and despair taken over your life? Do you ever find yourself wrestling with these negative thoughts:

- "Why am I the one to have such a terrible marriage?"
- "Everyone except me has a husband who talks to them."
- "There's no use in trying any further—our marriage is never going to change."

- "God has forgotten me."
- "Life just isn't fair."

These are sample doses of the toxic poison of self-pity. The only anti-dote we know to such misery and despair is praise and thanksgiving. Praise is, among other things, our vote that God is up to something good. It is a statement of faith that God is involved in my suffering, and it will end for my good and his glory. As the apostle Paul testi-fied, "Therefore we do not lose heart. Though outwardly we are wast-ing away, yet inwardly we are being renewed day by day. For our light and momentary troubles are achieving for us an eternal glory that far outweighs them all" (2 Corinthians 4:16-17).

Self-pity disappears when we follow the encouragement found in the Psalms:

> I will extol the LORD at all times;
> > his praise will always be on my lips.
> I will glory in the LORD;
> > let the afflicted hear and rejoice.
> Glorify the LORD with me;
> > let us exalt his name together.
> I sought the LORD, and he answered me;
> > he delivered me from all my fears.
> Those who look to him are radiant;
> > their faces are never covered with shame.
> > > (Psalm 34:1-5)

From Pity to Praise

Strange as it sounds, it is in the very depth of our misery and self-pity that we should begin to rejoice, exalt, and praise the name of Jesus Christ. The promise is God will answer us, he will deliver us from all our fears, our heart will experience a new radiance, and we will escape lasting shame. What might praise look like in your situation?

Lord Jesus, I rejoice and praise your magnificent name this day.
I thank you for your faithfulness, mercy, and love toward me. I

bless you because I believe this very day you are at work in my life and marriage. Though I may not see it at the moment, I trust your Word when it says you are working for my good and your glory. I believe this is true even in the problems I experience with my husband. I praise you for the man you gave me to spend my life with. I believe by faith that you have an eternal plan for this marriage to be fulfilling for both of us. Thank you for softening my heart toward my husband and for softening his heart toward me. In your powerful name, amen.

Jesus gave the man filled with self-pity a direct command to obey: "Get up! Pick up your mat and walk."

It is important that you leave your self-pity behind and be prepared to obey God as he leads you in getting your husband to talk.

5.

Have I been carrying resentment and bitterness toward my husband?

"I just can't forgive my husband," one wife in her late fifties tearfully explained to us, "not after the way he deceived me for so long." While he had stopped short of committing adultery, he had been involved in a number of emotional dalliances and then attempted to cover them up. "Not only that, but he rarely will talk to me when he is home. I fear he doesn't love me any longer."

It is understandable that a wife who has been betrayed by her husband would struggle with forgiveness, which is often both an event and a process. We make the definitive choice to cancel the moral debt owed us. Then we begin the difficult work of resolving the emotional pain and consequences it caused for us. That often goes hand in hand with the long and excruciating process of rebuilding trust.

Bitter Roots, Bitter Fruit

While there may be trust issues to resolve, and though it may take time to let go of hurt and wounded feelings, we dare not hold on to our bitterness and resentment. The Bible speaks plainly of dangerous consequences: "See to it that no one falls short of the grace of God and that no bitter root grows up to cause trouble and defile many" (Hebrews 12:15).

Let's assume for the moment we are not dealing with a serious offense, such as adultery or physical abuse, on the part of your husband. Let's assume your hurt and anger come from the fact he ignores you, seldom reciprocates affection, or sits in the living room all weekend watching games and says hardly a word to you.

While all these signs of rejection create emotional pain, if that pain has developed into heart-simmering anger, and if you have a desire to pay him back, then you have crossed the line into sin.

Bitterness is a settled decision not to forgive, and it builds enormous walls in relationships.

If your husband senses you still carry past grievances and are refusing to release him from the moral debt he owes you even though he has sought forgiveness, this is going to shut him down. Few people will continually approach a person for conversation when they know that person nurses grievances and resentments toward them. Bitter roots produce bitter fruits in a marriage.

Sensing bitterness, a husband will pull away from his wife, and if that goes on long enough, he may be tempted to seek emotional comfort from someone else. At best he will be reluctant to spend time together or engage in conversation.

One husband confessed, "She just refuses to forgive me for my past mistakes. Finally, I found someone at work who would listen to me. I didn't intend to have an emotional affair. I just needed someone to talk to who wasn't mad at me."

When I'm Good and Ready?

How can you know if you are harboring bitterness toward your husband? What are the warning signs of bitterness? Do you ever struggle with thoughts or emotions such as these?

- "I just wish someone would do to my husband what he's done to me."

- "I'll forgive him when I'm good and ready."
- "Until he changes, I'm not going to show him the respect he wants."
- "I wish sometimes he were dead and I could start my life over again."
- "I'm not giving him sex until he asks for forgiveness."

Unfortunately, there are dozens more such statements that reveal a bitter heart. (By the way, carrying bitterness toward anyone—your father, mother, siblings, children, past friends, or other believers—has the same final result of building a wall in your heart that shuts your husband out.)

The Bible teaches only one remedy for bitterness and that's forgiveness: "And do not grieve the Holy Spirit of God, with whom you were sealed for the day of redemption. Get rid of all bitterness, rage and anger, brawling and slander, along with every form of malice. Be kind and compassionate to one another, forgiving each other, just as in Christ God forgave you" (Ephesians 4:30-32).

Forgiveness Is a Choice, Not a Feeling

A couple sat in our office for several days without showing much physical affection for each other. The wife had been terribly wounded by her husband's behavior. It mirrored much of the same behavior she had seen in her father growing up. As the week of counseling wore on, she confessed she had never forgiven either her husband or her father.

We encouraged her to write down each instance in the past when either her husband or father had wounded her heart (that's not difficult for a person carrying bitterness). Then we encouraged her to pray the following prayer first shared with us by another pastor:

Lord, I choose to forgive my husband for ignoring me, causing me to feel sad, alone, rejected, and devalued. I am willing to bear the emotional pain and consequences that my husband has caused me and release it to you. I ask you, Lord, to take back the ground I gave to the enemy in my heart through my bitterness, and I yield that ground to your control. In your name, amen.

By the end of the week the couple was in each other's arms. The tears of forgiveness and healing flowed freely. The impact on the husband was immediate and profound. Now that the wall of bitterness had been torn down in his wife's heart, he felt a new freedom and desire to talk to her.

Releasing bitterness is simply a wise thing to do: "But the wisdom that comes from heaven is first of all pure; then peace-loving, considerate, submissive, full of mercy and good fruit, impartial and sincere. Peacemakers who sow in peace reap a harvest of righteousness" (James 3:17-18).

It may also get your husband to talk.

6.

Do I struggle with dark or evil thoughts toward my husband?

"I hate you! I hate you! I wish I had a gun and could shoot you!" The enraged wife slammed the door so hard leading to the garage that the glass shattered onto the driveway.

We wish we were making this up, but it happened, according to one husband who called our television program. The wife was a victim of severe emotional (and possibly sexual) abuse as a child. As an adult, she had been in and out of hospital treatment for clinical depression. One moment she was laughing and smiling, but if her husband said something that touched her pain, her visage would suddenly turn dark. The cruel (evil) words and behavior that would follow did enormous damage to her marriage and family.

When Darkness Descends

It would be tempting to simply assign such behavior to the aftereffects of severe abuse and trauma—and no doubt some of that was at play. Yet the Scriptures teach that it is also possible for a person to come under the influence of dark spirits that can seriously influence our personality and actions. Such instances are found throughout the New Testament. In fact Jesus frequently encountered people experiencing spiritual oppression during his earthly ministry:

> Just then a man in their synagogue who was possessed by an impure spirit cried out, "What do you want with us, Jesus of Nazareth? Have you come to destroy us? I know who you are—the Holy One of God!"
> "Be quiet!" said Jesus sternly. "Come out of him!" The impure spirit shook the man violently and came out of him with a shriek (Mark 1:23-26).

Can Christians Be Oppressed?

Let us be very clear that not everyone who struggles with difficult or dark thoughts is oppressed by an impure spirit. Christians cannot be possessed by evil spirits for the Holy Spirit lives in them. But it is possible for even believers to be influenced by evil: "Be alert and of sober mind. Your enemy the devil prowls around like a roaring lion looking for someone to devour" (1 Peter 5:8).

The Bible teaches it is possible for believers to end up deceived, doing the will of the evil one without realizing it:

> And the Lord's servant must not be quarrelsome but must be kind to everyone, able to teach, not resentful. Opponents must be gently instructed, in the hope that God will grant them repentance leading them to a knowledge of the truth, and that they will come to their senses and escape from the trap of the devil, who has taken them captive to do his will (2 Timothy 2:24-26).

Even the great apostle Peter, the same person Jesus just moments earlier had commended for his confession that Jesus is the Messiah, suddenly found himself under the influence of the evil one when Jesus predicted his own death and resurrection:

Peter took [Jesus] aside and began to rebuke him. "Never, Lord!" he said. "This shall never happen to you!"

Jesus turned and said to Peter, "Get behind me, Satan! You are a stumbling block to me; you do not have in mind the concerns of God, but merely human concerns" (Matthew 16:22-23).

While this discussion may sound "out there" to some of you, the Bible affirms that evil spirits can influence us. This doesn't mean that a wife is under the control of the devil because she momentarily entertains a cruel or wicked thought toward her husband. One of the devil's tactics is tempt us with horrible thoughts and then to accuse us for having those thoughts. In that case, we simply reject the thought as a lie from the father of lies and dismiss it.

Giving the Enemy an Open Door

Yet, if we have given ground to dark spirits or a place for them to operate, we can come under their influence. Erwin Lutzer, the gifted pastor of Moody Memorial Church in Chicago, describes how even believers can come under the influence of wrong spirits. In his ministry of helping people find spiritual freedom, he has found that spiritual oppression may enter through several doors:

1. We entertain a long-term sin such as bitterness.

2. We are abused or violated as children, and the trauma we experience opens our heart to a transmission of the evil from the offender to ourselves (such as in sexual abuse).

3. We inherit a generational bondage to a sin from our parents or grandparents who were involved in the occult.

4. We ourselves dabble in the occult in its many varieties.

5. We become heavily involved in a non-Christian teaching or religion that worships false gods.

Is it possible that you may have opened a door in your heart to the influence of dark forces opposed to Jesus Christ? That can certainly lead to both a spiritual and emotional barrier in your marriage.

The Author of Evil Thoughts

Do you ever struggle with thoughts similar to these?

- "I hate my husband. I know it's wrong, but I hate him anyway."
- "I wouldn't mind if he dropped dead tomorrow."
- "Maybe I should have an affair so I can teach him what it's like to hurt."
- "I hope he's not in heaven with me (or that he ends up in hell)."
- "Maybe I should just kill myself (or him) and leave all this pain behind."

Again, struggling momentarily with such thoughts is not proof-positive your heart is being oppressed by dark spirits. However, to have these thoughts reoccur is a danger sign since each of these statements reflects the agenda of our adversary: "The thief comes only to steal and kill and destroy; I have come that they may have life, and have it to the full" (John 10:10). If any of the thoughts you entertain regularly toward your husband include variations of stealing, killing, or destroying, you may be under spiritual attack.

We know of one couple where the wife had an affair because she kept having thoughts that her husband was unfaithful to her. It turns out he had been faithful to her all along, and she had been deceived into believing otherwise.

We should realize that our adversary can put evil thoughts in our mind, and then he tries to convince us they are our own. If you have ever struggled with dark or evil thoughts and wondered where such a wicked thought could come from, it may well be that the enemy has planted them.

What should you do if you find yourself struggling with such disturbing thoughts toward your husband? We have benefited much from the teaching of Neil Anderson, author of *The Bondage Breaker* (Harvest House Publishers, 2006). He suggests the solution is not having someone cast demons out of you, but for you to confess, renounce, and then resist these thoughts. They are not your thoughts and should be rejected as such. This principle is summarized in the book of James:

> Submit yourselves, then, to God. Resist the devil, and he will flee from you. Come near to God and he will come near to you. Wash your hands, you sinners, and purify your hearts, you double-minded. Grieve, mourn and wail. Change your laughter to mourning and your joy to gloom. Humble yourselves before the Lord, and he will lift you up (James 4:7-10).

A Prayer to Set You Free

If you are looking to find freedom from compulsive or obsessive thoughts or emotions, we suggest you pray a prayer similar to this (perhaps with a trusted prayer partner):

> *Dear Jesus, I confess that you are my Lord and Savior. You are Lord of lords and King of kings of this world and the universe. I praise and thank you that you achieved the final and complete victory over sin and darkness on the cross and disarmed all principalities and powers. Your resurrection is proof you have power even over death.*
>
> *I stand on that victory and authority as a member of your family of believers, and today I confess my involvement in [list any sins that could have opened the door to evil]. I believe your promise that "If we confess our sins, [you are] faithful and just and will forgive us our sins and purify us from all unrighteousness" (1 John 1:9).*
>
> *I renounce all ground I may have given to the enemy, and I submit my heart and life to you. In your name I resist the devil and all his forces. I choose this day forward to live in obedience*

to your will, Lord Jesus. Thank you for the freedom you purchased for me with your precious blood. In your name and authority I pray, amen.

If you have been struggling with spiritual oppression and you confess, renounce, and resist the sins that have plagued you, then you should begin to feel both peace and joy entering your life again. Whenever temptation comes knocking, simply take your stand based on your position in Christ: *Lord, as a child of God, I renounce and resist this temptation and submit my heart and mind to your total control.*

The Weapon the Enemy Fears Most

Never forget as well the power of the memorized Word of God to help you achieve daily victory. One of the passages of Scripture Bob learned as a child has proven to be a powerful weapon in winning the battle when our enemy attacks: "No temptation has overtaken you except what is common to man. And God is faithful; he will not let you be tempted beyond what you can bear. But when you are tempted, he will also provide a way out so that you can endure it" (1 Corinthians 10:13).

It's an excellent and powerful verse to claim when struggling with intense emotions or angry thoughts toward your husband. God has promised to always offer you a way of escape from thoughts or feelings that threaten to overwhelm your heart or ruin your marriage.

Think of the authority of God's Word as the Plexiglas barrier you find at a zoo. The lion or tiger behind that clear but solid wall may offer a menacing growl or even charge you, but the wall stops him in his tracks.

Jesus held up the Word of God when the devil confronted him in the wilderness: "Jesus answered, '[God's Word says]: "Do not put the Lord your God to the test."' When the devil had finished all this tempting, he left him until an opportune time" (Luke 4:12-13).

The enemy was beaten, and Jesus walked away victorious. The same can be true in your marriage. As you confess, renounce, and resist the spiritual issues in your life, the barriers in your heart between you and your husband collapse.

Does the Holy Spirit Have All of You?

Not only is it necessary to resist the temptation of dark spirits, it's vitally important to pray daily for the filling of the Holy Spirit. While all believers receive all of the Holy Spirit the day they become a Christian, that doesn't mean the Holy Spirit necessarily receives all of us. We can end up holding things back from God's control. Part of us remains under the control of what the Bible calls our flesh or sinful nature: "The acts of the flesh are obvious: sexual immorality, impurity and debauchery; idolatry and witchcraft; hatred, discord, jealousy, fits of rage, selfish ambition, dissensions, factions and envy; drunkenness, orgies, and the like" (Galatians 5:19-21).

Allowing our sinful nature to influence us can cause problems in our close relationships: "And do not grieve the Holy Spirit of God, with whom you were sealed for the day of redemption. Get rid of all bitterness, rage and anger, brawling and slander, along with every form of malice" (Ephesians 4:30-31).

Amazing isn't it? We can bring deep grief and sorrow to the Spirit of God when we display bitterness, rage, anger, and fighting in our marriage. That's why we should pray daily, *Lord Jesus, take complete control of my life. Fill me with your Holy Spirit this day so that all my words, actions, and motives will glorify you.*

Living your life daily under the control of the Holy Spirit will have an amazing impact on your marriage: "But the fruit of the Spirit is love, joy, peace, forbearance, kindness, goodness, faithfulness, gentleness and self-control...Since we live by the Spirit, let us keep in step with the Spirit" (Galatians 5:22-23,25).

As your husband begins to see your newfound spiritual joy and freedom, it will intrigue him, and he may wish to talk to you to find out just what happened.

Step Three: Trust Christ and make a full surrender of your life and marriage.

The final step in preparation for getting your husband to talk is to make a full surrender of your life and marriage to God's loving and sovereign control. The Bible promises if we do that, God's will for us will come into crystal clear focus:

> Therefore, I urge you, brothers and sisters, in view of God's mercy, to offer your bodies as a living sacrifice, holy and pleasing to God—this is your true and proper worship. Do not conform to the pattern of this world, but be transformed by the renewing of your mind. Then you will be able to test and approve what God's will is—his good, pleasing and perfect will (Romans 12:1-3).

Victory Through Surrender

How do we do that in a practical sense? Let's go back to the Serenity Prayer we discussed in an earlier chapter:

> *God grant me the serenity to accept the things I cannot change; courage to change the things I can; and wisdom to know the difference. Living one day at a time; enjoying one moment at a time; accepting hardships as the pathway to peace; taking as [Jesus] did, this sinful world as it is, not as I would have it; trusting that he will make all things right if I surrender to his will; that I may be reasonably happy in this life and supremely happy with him forever in the next. Amen.*

This simple prayer contains a wealth of important biblical principles for surrendering our lives to the control, care, and direction of our heavenly Father.

First, we are to ask for peace of mind for the things we cannot change. The Scriptures promise,

> You will keep in perfect peace
> those whose minds are steadfast,
> because they trust in you.
>   (Isaiah 26:3)

You need to turn over to God's control the issues in your marriage that you cannot alter or change—including whether your husband chooses to talk to you.

Second, we are to ask for courage to change the things we can. Again, the Scriptures have wonderful assurance for us to lean on: "Have I not commanded you? Be strong and courageous. Do not be afraid; do not be discouraged, for the LORD your God will be with you wherever you go" (Joshua 1:9). This book is all about having the courage to do the things you can to get your husband to talk to you. Thankfully, you don't have to do that all on your own. If you surrender your life to God's will, he will provide you with that courage when you need it.

Third, we are to ask for the wisdom to know the difference between the things we cannot change and the things we can. Wisdom is the application of truth to our lives in a way that honors God. If we aren't sure whether we should accept our circumstances with serenity or exercise the courage to change them, we can ask God for the wisdom to know which to do. Our heavenly Father is more than willing to provide us with an answer: "If any of you lacks wisdom, you should ask God, who gives generously to all without finding fault, and it will be given to you" (James 1:5). Should you suggest to your husband that together you seek help for your marriage? Or would it better to wait on that? You can bring such questions to God, and he will generously answer.

Fourth, we are to live one day and one moment at a time. When you surrender your life and marriage to God, he takes responsibility for your future. All the questions you may have about tomorrow, God has already answered: "But seek first his kingdom and his righteousness, and all these things will be given to you as well. Therefore do not worry about tomorrow, for tomorrow will worry about itself. Each day has enough trouble of its own" (Matthew 6:33-34). Don't let your life be consumed by all the what-ifs in getting your husband to talk—leave those contingencies with God.

Fifth, we are to accept life as it is, not as we wish it to be. Our world is filled with disappointment, hardships, and yes—sin. We can either let that discourage and disillusion us, or we can believe these difficulties are accomplishing a far greater eternal purpose in our lives:

Therefore we do not lose heart. Though outwardly we are wasting away, yet inwardly we are being renewed day by day. For our light and momentary troubles are achieving for us an eternal glory that far outweighs them all. So we fix our eyes not on what is seen, but on what is unseen, since what is seen is temporary, but what is unseen is eternal (2 Corinthians 4:16-18).

Even if you wish your marriage were different than it is, you can still rest in the fact that God is at work accomplishing something of eternal importance in you.

Sixth, we are to trust that he will make all things right if we surrender to his will. Jesus is our example of patiently enduring the injustices of life, knowing that God will ultimately make all things right.

To this you were called, because Christ suffered for you, leaving you an example, that you should follow in his steps.
"He committed no sin,
and no deceit was found in his mouth."
When they hurled their insults at him, he did not retaliate; when he suffered, he made no threats. Instead, he entrusted himself to him who judges justly (1 Peter 2:21-23).

Your husband may have said things to you he should not have said. He may have ignored you in a way that he should not have. He may now be resistant to talking to you about things he should talk to you about. Don't let such disappointment or hurt capture your soul—entrust it all to God. He has pledged to ultimately make all things right.

Finally, we are to adjust our expectations to be reasonably happy in this life and supremely happy in the eternal life to come. This is not a perfect world, nor will it be until Christ returns to establish his eternal kingdom. That doesn't mean we simply endure life until it ends; rather, we find our contentment in our relationship with Christ.

I am not saying this because I am in need, for I have learned to be content whatever the circumstances. I know what it is to be in need, and I know what it is to have plenty. I have learned the secret of being content in any and every situation, whether well fed or hungry, whether living in plenty or in want. I can do all this through him who gives me strength (Philippians 4:11-13).

Make Me an Instrument of Your Peace

It is vitally important as you begin this journey of getting your husband to talk that he sense in you serenity, courage, and wisdom. Even if your relationship with your husband is not where you want it to be nor progressing in the direction you desire, by learning the secret of contentment in Christ, you can be at peace.

When you are at peace, it will have an impact on your husband. He will notice and ultimately respond to the difference he sees in you. While it may not get him to talk all at once, it will create a new dynamic between the two of you. If nothing else, he will want to talk to you about what's happened in your life. As Gary Chapman says, while you cannot change your spouse, you can influence him—and a heart at peace with God is a great influencer.

Now that we've looked at how you can prepare your own heart for God to work in your marriage, let's look in the next chapter at one last question: how can I know that my efforts to get my husband to talk to me are truly working? The answers may not be as obvious as you think.

Questions to Consider

1. Why is it important that your heart be right with God before undertaking the journey of getting your husband to talk? What could potentially go wrong if your heart is not right with Christ? Are you certain that you are going to heaven? Do you know how you would answer the two questions on p. 108? According to John 1:12-13 and John 3:16, how does a person receive the gift of eternal life? Have you taken that step of saving faith?

2. What is the value of taking a searching spiritual and emotional inventory of your life for your marriage? As you go down the list of six questions in the spiritual inventory section, do you see ones you must answer yes? Can you see how these could keep your husband from talking? How can the prayer of Psalm 19:12-13 become a blessing in your life? Would you be willing to go down that list of questions with a trusted, kind, and honest friend and ask her if she sees any at work in your life?

3. What are the real dangers of allowing bitterness to take root in our lives, according to Hebrews 12:15? Are there subtle shoots of bitterness growing in the soil of your marriage? Are you willing to make a list of all the people, including family members and spouse, who have hurt you? Are you willing to forgive each person and each offense one by one? How could freedom from bitterness be used by God to get your husband to talk?

4. Does the Bible say it is possible for Christians to be oppressed (not possessed) by dark spirits? What does 2 Timothy 2:24-26 have to say on that subject? Do you ever have thoughts toward your husband or other people that you don't believe come from you? Why is it important you actively confess, renounce, and resist dark impulses? How can memorizing 1 Corinthians 10:13 give you victory when you're tempted to feel anger, bitterness, or worse toward your husband?

5. Why is it important to make a full surrender of your life to Christ before you take on the challenge of getting your husband to talk? How did Jesus make a complete surrender of his life in the Garden of Gethsemane, as recorded in Luke 22:39-46? Are you prepared to say the same things he did? What if God's will for your life is different from what you asked for—are you still willing to accept that?

6. How can learning the Serenity Prayer help you find peace in the midst of troubling circumstances? Why are serenity,

courage, and wisdom important in preparing your heart to get your husband to talk? What harm will worry, fear, and foolishness do to your relationship? How can Philippians 4:4-7 prepare you to face an uncertain future as you begin the journey of getting your husband to talk?

7. Should finding happiness be the ultimate goal of a marriage? If not, what should be our goal according to Colossians 1:9-10? How could a focus on pleasing the Lord eventually produce happiness in your marriage?

6

How to Know It's Working

"The people were amazed when they saw the mute
speaking...And they praised the God of Israel."

MATTHEW 15:31

One wife who took our advice to ask her husband meaningful, non-threatening questions and to allow him to talk uninterrupted and without judgment wrote to tell us she had a new problem. Her husband was now calling her twice a day and talking for an hour each time (he used to call only once a week and then to talk only to the kids).

"Just keep doing what you're doing," we said.

Like any major change that enters our lives, adapting to a new reality can be difficult—even if it is what we've always wanted. Ask the spouse of someone who is now free from alcohol or drug addiction. You'll hear that, along with their thanksgiving, they now have a new set of problems to solve—albeit good ones—because their life has radically changed.

We enjoy southern gospel hymns because of their typically positive message. One of our favorites is "The Baptism of Jesse Taylor." The gist of the song is that Jesse Taylor, a local legend for his drinking, gambling, and womanizing, met Jesus and has become a changed man, creating an entirely new reality for the law, his neighbors, and his wife and their little son. (You can read the song lyrics at www.cowboylyrics.com/lyrics/oak-ridge-boys/the-baptism-of-jesse-taylor-12746.html.)

When a husband changes, everything around him typically begins to change. That's the considerable spiritual influence God has given to men.

How can you know if your husband has undergone a change of heart? *Well, won't he just start talking?* Yes, but this means more than just increasing his quantity of words. If your husband has changed, something important has transpired—he has chosen to open his heart to you and that will show.

You will know your husband has opened his heart to you when several of the following begin to happen in your relationship.

---

1. He will call or communicate with you more often during the day.

Perhaps he used to call only when he was leaving work or briefly during lunch to discuss primarily family business matters. You will know he has changed when he calls just to call you—just to connect with you. Yes, it may still involve the kids, bills, and what's for supper, but he'll enjoy hearing your voice, and there will be an emotional connection between you.

One wife, whose husband underwent a profound change of heart after she began listening to him and discovered the deep source of his pain that went back decades, told us, "I have a new husband. He calls me all the time. To tell you the truth, I can't even show others what he texts me."

---

2. He will tell you things you never knew about him.

One of the surest signs that your husband is now opening his heart to you is the revelation of new information from his past. We're not talking about confessing some scandalous or immoral episode (though in some cases that may need to occur). What he's more likely to talk about are things from his past that he never felt free to share.

Randy began telling his wife, Sharon, about the deep pain his brother Jack's troubled marriage had caused him as a child. He recounted all the days as a boy he had watched his mother cry at the dinner table. He shared how painful it was to visit Jack's home as his angry wife, Theresa, would openly ridicule Christianity and her in-laws for practicing their faith, such as tithing to the church.

What Sharon discovered was that Randy grew up wounded and confused and angry. He confessed resentment toward Jack for bringing such a difficult person into their family. As Randy talked, he walked Sharon right to the door of the pain in his heart. "I feel that I was robbed of a childhood. All the emotional energy and attention in our family went to trying to rescue my brother. I felt ignored at times because all the focus was on his latest drama."

Not all the information your husband will begin to share will be necessarily negative or painful. He may tell you about funny episodes from his past, such as the time the family dog stole a baked chicken from the table while everyone was bowed in prayer.

Husbands have a lot to talk about if given the chance.

---

3. He will make the conversations last longer.

You may be used to a conversation that lasts only a minute or two (unless an argument breaks out). One of the signs that you are getting him to open his heart to you is that he'll stay engaged in the conversation for longer and longer periods of time.

The late author and philosopher Francis Schaeffer and his wife operated a retreat center in Switzerland for several decades. He recounted how a young wife and husband came to stay with them. After working through their issues and finding a new spiritual connection with God and each other, the couple stayed up night after night just talking to each other. Because it was close quarters, other retreat residents could overhear these two conversing long into the night. While perhaps irritating, it was a sure sign that something had changed for the good in their marriage.

The longer your husband is willing to talk to you, the more it means that he feels he is connecting with you.

4. He will show his emotions and feelings in your presence.

Over time, a husband who is opening his heart to you will begin taking chances to display his emotions in front of you. Not that he will begin weeping every day, but you will see much more variety and intensity to his feelings than before (almost all to the good).

When we had to put down Boaz, the beloved collie who belonged to our middle son, Brent, Bob was rather stoic. While Brent was away in the army, the dog lost the use of his back legs, which set in motion a series of other health issues. Bob was away speaking the day Cheryl and another son took our dog to the veterinarian for the last time. When Bob came home, he bravely acknowledged the loss, and a few days later began giving away the remaining dog food, collars, and leashes to friends. Outwardly he was doing fine, until the day a small box arrived from the veterinarian's office. When Bob unwrapped the box, inside was a carefully wrapped plaster cast of Boaz's final footprint.

That was it. Bob was undone. "I don't know if I can keep this; it's just too painful," he later confided to Cheryl.

When a husband begins to show his deeper emotions in front of his wife, particularly those feelings that express sorrow and loss, it's a sign that he is now talking to his wife on a heart level. That is a level reserved for her and no one else.

For some wives, seeing their husbands begin to show deeper emotions can be unsettling. Perhaps she's used to the stoic, stone-faced husband. She need not fear, however, that his display of emotions is a sign he's falling apart. Rather, it's a sign that he's beginning to trust her on a new level.

When he does show emotion, what should a wife do? Simply hold him and let him say whatever he needs to say. The less you say probably the better. What he needs is your love, hugs, encouragement, and honor spoken without words.

5. He will be more openly affectionate and say he loves you more often.

Bob does a weekly television call-in program that deals with marriage problems. (*Marriage: For Better, For Worse* can be viewed on Mondays at noon and at 9:00 p.m. central time by going to www.tln.com and clicking on the link, "To Watch Online.") One evening a woman called who had heard Bob say that most husbands are lonely and long for a companion. She had taken our advice to heart to go along with her husband on simple errands so he wouldn't have to go alone.

"Pastor Bob," she said excitedly, "it works! The other day my husband announced, 'I'm going to Home Depot and I'll be back in an hour or so.' That's when I saw my chance. I said, 'Can I go with you?' 'You want to go to Home Depot with me?' he said. 'Sure, why not? Let's go.' Well, we got to the store and he began explaining all the different tools and parts. Right in the middle of the aisle he suddenly wheeled around, wrapped his arms around me, and said, 'I love you so much.' Pastor Bob, we were right in the middle of the plumbing aisle, and my husband is holding me tight and telling me he loves me! Can you believe that?"

"Yes," Bob said. "And I know why he did that. You entered his world, you were his companion, you were willing to talk about the things that interest him, and he felt close to you and he started talking to you."

You Will Hear the Words "I Love You"

We'll say it again—as you get your husband to talk to you, he is going to feel closer and closer to you. As this continues, the day will come where all on his own, without reminder or coercion, he will say, "I love you." In fact, he will begin to say it more and more because he means it.

Instead of responding, "Well, finally!" or "Oh, you can actually say those words," we recommend you simply smile and say, "Thank you. I love you too."

---

6. He will talk to you during sex more than he used to.

Perhaps your husband has been largely silent during sex. Perhaps apart from a moment of ecstasy, your husband ordinarily says little or nothing to you. Once the act is over (as far as he is concerned), he simply rolls over and goes to sleep or gets up and leaves the room—and you are left feeling unfulfilled and all alone.

As you get him to talk outside the bedroom, he will begin talking to you more inside the bedroom.

He may begin by expressing how much he enjoys sex with you. He will likely progress to telling you how attractive you are. Finally, he will start saying how much he loves you. God designed the sexual act so that a married couple would look into each other's eyes and share themselves heart-to-heart, soul-to-soul, and body-to-body.

If your husband is talking to you more during the day, he will begin talking to you more once sex is completed. The more you respond to him by expressing your admiration, respect, and gratitude for his lovemaking, the more likely it is he will stay with you and talk. This will help fulfill your need for a social and emotional connection that makes the sexual act much more meaningful to you.

---

7. He will find excuses just to be with you.

One wife told us with obvious satisfaction that, as the result of the new heart connection, "My husband never leaves me alone. He follows me everywhere at home. I can't get away from the man!"

This may be more the exception than the rule. Not every wife is going to find herself followed by her husband wherever she goes. However, a husband who is talking to his wife because she listens to his heart is going to find excuses to be with her. He may leave for work a few minutes later than usual or he may arrive home sooner than expected. If his business trip ends early, he will take an earlier flight home and surprise you. While you are swimming in the pool, you may find him standing at the other end holding out a rose for you.

One older couple had built over the decades an incredibly strong marriage and heart connection, and the wife told us, "He just doesn't want to go anywhere by himself. He misses me too much. Even on his summer fishing trips, he won't go unless I'm willing to go with him." The book of Proverbs speaks to such a connection:

> A man wandering from his home
> is like a bird wandering from its nest.
> (Proverbs 27:8 HCSB)

We've said, as a general rule, that men will seek out places where they are respected, listened to, and not judged. For some males, that place is the local shooting range or hunt club; for others it's a sports bar or night club; and for others it's a gym or athletic league. Our encouragement is to make your home the place your husband seeks out to be heard and respected.

Martin Luther, once a committed single man who later married and enjoyed a deep and satisfying relationship with his wife, wrote, "There is no more lovely, friendly, and charming relationship, communion, or company than a good marriage." When a man feels that way about his wife, he will find any excuse to be with her.

---

8. He will have eyes for you only.

The husband who looks at or ogles other women often does so because he is looking for a heart connection, though he doesn't realize it (this is an explanation, not an excuse). He is, as one marriage counselor puts it, "sexualizing his feelings of loneliness."

When men feel emotionally distant, alone, and even estranged from their wife, it can open them up to the temptation to find a heart connection elsewhere. That's when they may be tempted to begin hanging out with mixed company from the office after work. That's when they start staying out late on business dinners while their wife waits for them at home. That's when they start emailing other female acquaintances.

Note: we are not for a moment blaming the sinful behavior of these men on the failings of their spouse—every wife has the right to expect her husband to honor his wedding vows to "forsake all others."

However, if a wife has inadvertently put up heart barriers, withheld sex for leverage, overwhelmed her husband with unrealistic expectations, or made it difficult for him to express his true feelings and thoughts, it can contribute to the setup for an emotional or even physical affair.

If a wife accepts her husband as he is, refuses to judge or criticize his innermost thoughts, and makes it easy for him to share his feelings, it is more than likely he will have eyes only for her.

One husband who enjoyed a strong marriage told us of a business trip he was once on. He was headed up to his hotel room, and just as the elevator doors were closing, two women stepped aboard and said, "Do you like pretty girls?"

"Yes, I definitely do," he said. "And I have one waiting for me at home."

The two women got off the elevator as quickly as they could.

---

9. He will be more peaceful about his life.

A sure sign that your husband is opening his heart to you is that he will express satisfaction with his life. This goes back to a man's basic need for tranquility, which we discussed in an earlier chapter. Bob once asked a roomful of husbands if they had a deep need for peace and serenity in their lives. Virtually every man in the room raised his hand.

As your husband begins talking to you, you will discover the things that bring his heart greater contentment and calm. You will become his "safe place" to bring his worries and concerns to.

We once saw a segment on a television newsmagazine that featured a high-strung executive in a pressure-filled environment. The stress ultimately resulted in a heart attack. After nearly dying, this man knew he had to make radical changes in his life. That's when he and his wife struck on a novel idea. He moved a second desk for her right into his office and invited her to come to work with him each day. A reporter asked him how this was working out.

"Wonderful," he said. "Now whenever I get overstressed, I just stop and talk to her about it for a few minutes. Then I feel much better and I get back to work."

Regardless of whether such a model could be implemented in your husband's workplace, the principle is obvious—if he can openly discuss his pressures and concerns with you, he is going to enjoy a more peaceful and less anxious life.

---

10. He will pray and read the Scriptures with you.

One couple who sought help came to us with their marriage on life support. They were so frustrated in their attempts to communicate that they had even resorted to throwing shoes at each other (a different sort of "sole mate," you might say).

Through our weeklong pastoral care sessions, the husband began to talk and open his heart to his wife, and a most unexpected thing happened. When they entered our office at the end of the week, they were holding hands and smiling. Once they were seated, the wife looked at her husband and said, "Dear, why don't you read what you read to me from the Bible this morning? It was so amazing," Obviously enjoying her compliment, he opened his big Bible and read to us all.

That has turned out not to be an isolated incident. We have heard from other couples that one of the unexpected results of a husband now talking openly and honestly with his wife is his newfound desire to pray and read Scripture with her.

This really shouldn't surprise anyone. God designed the husband to serve as the spiritual leader in a marriage and to love his wife with a Christlike love:

> Husbands, love your wives, just as Christ loved the church
> and gave himself up for her to make her holy, cleansing
> her by the washing with water through the word, and to
> present her to himself as a radiant church, without stain or
> wrinkle or any other blemish, but holy and blameless. In
> this same way, husbands ought to love their wives as their
> own bodies. He who loves his wife loves himself (Ephe-
> sians 5:25-28).

One application in everyday life is for the husband to read the Scriptures to his wife. For wives who yearn for their husband to take on the role of the spiritual leader and have hinted, cajoled, and even begged him to do so without success, simply listening to him in a sincere, patient, and nonjudgmental fashion may finally produce that result. There are no guarantees, but when a Christian husband feels respected and understood, he will begin to desire to connect with his wife spiritually through reading the Word and praying together.

Conclusion

Bob experienced a dramatic encounter with God during his second year of seminary, and that experience gave him a deeper level of peace and contentment than he had ever known before. During Christmas break, one of his college friends met him for coffee and concluded their time together by saying, "Robert, you've changed. You're not the same person. Something has changed in you."

When something happens in the heart of a man, it isn't long until others notice.

When a new and meaningful heart connection occurs between a husband and wife, it won't be long until others notice—particularly the wife. He will show less tension, demonstrate more patience, and ultimately display a more loving heart. If your husband is talking to you because he's opening his heart to you on a deeper level, you won't need anyone to tell you. You will know it's working.

After such a breakthrough had taken place in their marriage, one couple wrote us, "At least twelve couples have asked us what has happened to our marriage. They want to know if the same thing can happen in theirs."

The answer is yes. And it can happen in yours as well.

Questions to Consider

1. What changes in your husband's heart would convince you something has changed? How did the people know God had done a great work in the life of the apostle Paul, according to Galatians 1:22-24? If your husband begins to talk to you, will that require some adjustments on your part? Could any of those adjustments be potentially awkward or difficult?

2. Why would your husband want to communicate with you

more often once he feels drawn to you? Why might he be avoiding that now? According to Proverbs 27:9, what type of friend offers heartfelt advice? Are you a pleasant person to talk to?

3. How have you responded in the past to your husband when he has shown sorrow or tears? What truth did people conclude from Jesus's open display of emotions in John 11:35-36? Are you prepared to respect, honor, and comfort your husband if he were to open up his emotions to you?

4. Why is it easier to say "I love you" to someone you feel connected to? How does the spouse in Song of Songs 4:1-7 speak to his wife? Would you enjoy hearing such words from your husband? Do you tell him often that you love him?

5. Is it possible that men who look at other women (ungodly as that behavior is) are actually searching for an emotional connection? How is looking each other in the eyes an indication of emotional intimacy in a marriage? What did Jesus say about the importance of the eyes in Luke 11:34?

6. Do you believe God designed husbands to provide spiritual leadership and for wives to respond in spiritual followership? How is the model of Christ and the church found in Ephesians 5:25-33 a design for marriage? What would it mean to you to have your husband read the Scriptures to you and pray with you daily?

7

Answering the Most Common Questions

*"I would state my case before him
and fill my mouth with arguments.
I would find out what he would answer me,
and consider what he would say to me."*

JOB 23:4-5

Wives who read our advice on how to get their husband to talk often have a number of immediate questions they would like answered. In order to help them with their concerns, we've provided here our answers to the most common questions and objections.

Question 1: In our marriage I'm the quiet one and he's the talkative one. How would you help us?

If you are the one who typically keeps silent and buries things deep within your heart, it is vitally important that your husband gets you to talk to him sooner or later. He needs to read this book and learn the principles that will get you to talk. Not everything that works for him as a man will translate to you as a woman. Yet, there will be many areas of overlap that will help get you to talk.

Women can hesitate to talk for many of the same reasons men do. For example, a wife may be naturally shy, lack the self-confidence to share her feelings for fear of rejection, or she has been so wounded by her past it is simply too painful to talk about. Some wives are married to an expressive and dominating husband who overwhelms them. They have learned to become emotionally submissive and "go along to get along."

Please realize there is a world of difference between spiritual submission and emotional submission. Spiritual submission is when wives "voluntarily yield in love," which biblically is the right thing to do. That is, you are to show your husband honor and respect in his role as the spiritual leader of the family. Emotional submission is when wives choose to simply "go along to get along," to avoid conflict or adverse reactions, even when his behavior or conduct is less than right and warrants you drawing a boundary. Such emotional submission is the wrong thing to do.

Tired of Going Along to Get Along

If you find yourself outwardly complying but inwardly reacting to your husband, there's a real danger that someday your marriage is going to self-destruct.

How does that happen? The day finally arrives (perhaps after years or even decades) when you can no longer "go along to get along." All the years of denying your true feelings and simply bowing and complying with the will of others to avoid rejection finally takes its toll on your heart. You "flip" (as one writer puts it) and go from an emotionally submissive to an emotionally dominant person. The Teddy Bear has become the Grizzly Bear. The husband is shell-shocked by the drastic changes, the kids are caught off guard, and friends say they no longer recognize the person they once knew.

Rather than allow that sad scenario to play out in your life someday, we suggest instead that you communicate your true feelings to your husband now, perhaps in the presence of a counselor or pastor. You may need to tell your spouse after years of never consulting you before a decision, or just expecting you to go along with whatever he decides to do, that you need to express yourself.

If your husband is to respond correctly, he will need to display the same attitudes and practice the same skills we suggest for wives whose husbands will not talk. In other words, he should ask such questions as, "What's going on in your heart that you wish someone knew about?" or "How can I care about the pain you are carrying?"

He will need to listen with the sole purpose of understanding your heart better than he has in the past. He will need to give you long and uninterrupted opportunities to talk and stifle any inclination to criticize, demean, or devalue what you are saying. He will need to ask clarifying questions rather than offering condemning opinions.

Speaking from Your Heart

But what if he is unresponsive or tone-deaf to the unmet needs in your heart?

You need to be prepared to be honest with your husband and share with him the reasons you don't talk to him. If you are an emotionally submissive person, you may need to write a letter like this to him:

> Dear, I need to share with you some very important information about me. There are some things I need to say that I may have never said to you before. There will be a time and place for me to hear your heart, but for the moment I need you to hear mine.
>
> I grew up with a message communicated to me loud and clear—my thoughts and feelings were better kept to myself to avoid upsetting someone else. As I grew older I learned to outwardly comply, but inwardly I was reacting. I would often go along to get along. I found I could keep other people happy if I didn't say what I was thinking nor did what I really wanted to do. The result was I said yes when so often I wanted to say no. I let others do all the talking and kept my thoughts inside—often burying my emotions deep inside my heart.
>
> I regret to say that I brought this heart damage to our marriage. I wanted to make you happy and avoid rejection, so I decided to continue doing what I had learned to do so

well—to say yes when I really meant no (or the other way around). But the result of all this is that I have been frustrated, at other times angry, and still at other times shut down. That's why I quit talking. I struggle with feelings of despair that the rest of my life will continue like this, and sometimes I feel trapped.

I am committed to our marriage and to living the rest of my life with you just as I vowed the day we married. What I need from you are opportunities to share what's on my heart without you evaluating, criticizing, or rejecting what I've just said. When you ask me if I want to do something or go somewhere, and I say yes or no, I need you to ask, "Is that what you really want to do—really?" or "Is that what you really mean?"

After years of suppressing my true thoughts or desires, it may take me some time to learn to be bold enough to ask for what I truly need or say what I truly mean. I was not deliberately deceiving you or anyone else—I was just too insecure to take the risk of displeasing you or others. So I told you what I thought you wanted to hear, or I did what I thought you wanted me to do. Instead, I should have been practicing what the Bible calls "speaking the truth in love."

Please understand I'm not asking to always have my way. I'm not saying I should always say whatever is on my mind. Rather, I am telling you that I need you to listen to me—to ask me questions, to give me your focused attention, and let me share my heart with you. My pledge to you is that if you are willing to love me in this way by listening to me, I will seek to listen to your heart as well.

I ask your forgiveness for giving you the impression that all was well with me when it was not. My desire going forward is that I would share the real me and know the real you—without us judging or trying to change one another. Let's have a marriage where we share our secrets with each other. Let's connect our hearts for a lifetime. That's my true desire. Thank you for listening. I love you.

One way or another, you need to tell your husband that you need to talk and that remaining quiet and going along is not working. Just as it is vital to the future of a marriage for a wife to get her husband to talk, it is vital for your husband to get you to talk.

Question 2: What if my husband tells me about serious problems, and I don't know what to do with them (such as a pornography addiction, past infidelities, major depression, or even suicidal thoughts)?

One of the greatest motivations for a husband to keep quiet is the fear that if he shares what's in his heart, his wife may not be able to handle it. He worries that she may lose it, hold it against him for the rest of their lives, or worst of all choose to leave him.

The deciding factor for many husbands is, *Will she accept me or will she judge me for what I tell her?* If he has felt judged, evaluated, or criticized for what he has said in past conversations, he will be reluctant to take the chance again. Or if growing up he was told to shut up or sit down or go away, he will be hesitant as an adult to speak his true feelings and thoughts.

Choose Your Reaction in Advance

That is why it is all important that you decide ahead of time, *Whatever my husband tells me, I will respond with calm, grace, respect, and acceptance.* If he senses you are willing to listen without criticizing him, then little by little he is going to open up to you. You don't need to wait for the "big talk" to start demonstrating this new approach toward him. Perhaps you should communicate the following:

> It is more important that you share with me your true feelings and thoughts rather than tell me what you think I want to hear or will make me happy. I want you to know that whatever you tell me, I will treat you with respect and won't judge you for it. In fact, I will take it as a sign that you trust me and desire to be close to me.

If you feel you need to take this step, it's important to determine your attitude and response prior to learning something that could be potentially upsetting. For example, we've already discussed how important it is that you not overreact if your husband shares something difficult to hear, such as a struggle with pornography. While the news could feel earthshattering, he is not telling you this in order to destroy you. He is likely telling you because he is burdened, afraid, and desperate. He is calling out to you as a drowning man pleading for a life preserver.

While your first instinct might be to burst into tears or go into an emotional tailspin or even lash out at him, ask God for the strength and wisdom to resist doing so. There will be a time and a place to allow your damaged heart to cry out and your wounded emotions to flow freely, but now is likely not that moment. Drawing upon all the inner strength and composure God can give you, perhaps say,

> That must have taken a great deal of courage for you to tell me this, and I thank you for trusting me enough to share your struggle. I am your wife and friend and ally, and together with God's help, we will conquer this together. Though you can understand why I struggle with this news, I still respect and honor you as my husband. Perhaps we can stop right now and pray together about what first steps we will take to help you break free.

We know we are asking a lot of you to respond in such a gracious fashion. We do not for a moment underestimate the depth of shock or dismay you may be feeling.

Even when the news is difficult, please remember he is now honestly talking to you—what you have always desired.

Implementing the Buddy System

When Bob attended summer camp as a child, the camp used the buddy system to prevent drowning during swim times. The concept was simple—each camper was assigned a buddy who would stay close to them while in the pool or lake. That way, no one could go under without someone noticing immediately.

Our plea is to implement the buddy system in your marriage. Take a step back from the heartbreaking news and attempt to see yourself for the moment as your husband's buddy rather than his spouse. He may be drowning in a sin or a habit he can't break, and he needs someone to notice and come to his aid.

A man will likely tell his hidden sins to a close friend he trusts, whereas he may not tell his wife. But if he senses that you are not only his wife but also his buddy, he may open up to you. While a buddy might feel disappointment in his friend for his involvement in pornography, he would likely not cry or condemn but rather express compassion and support. He is there to help rescue not reject.

A Cry for Help

It may be asking too much for you to withhold tears and anguish when you learn your husband has a pornography problem, but if you can accept that he is telling you this to save your marriage not destroy it, and that it is a plea for help, it may help soften your response. Remember, the first words out of your mouth after such a revelation will have a great impact on the future of your relationship.

Some husbands may reveal such information simply as a prelude to say they are no longer in love and are leaving the marriage. Yet let's assume that your husband's motive in telling you about his problem is not to end the marriage but to try and rebuild it based on the truth rather than a deception. Please remember what Scripture tells us about those who desire to come clean and make past wrongs right:

> Whoever conceals their sins does not prosper,
>> but the one who confesses and renounces them finds
>>> mercy.
>> (Proverbs 28:13)

Now let's assume the problem is worse than pornography. Perhaps he is approaching you to confess his involvement in an emotional or physical affair. This likely takes things to a higher level than that of a pornography addiction. While pornography is an adultery-like act, the actual act of adultery where physical intimacy occurs is a game-changer.

If your husband were to confess, for the purposes of renouncing, past infidelity, what would he receive from you? Would he find mercy or condemnation?

You Can't Love an Image

We know of a man who finally admitted to his wife that he had visited prostitutes earlier in his life. While initially shocked, angered, and shaken, once this wife had time to process this information, and realized he was trying to rebuild the relationship rather than destroy it, she chose to pursue reconciliation with her husband. They were able to renew their vows and begin a new marriage.

Why was it necessary for him to confess the truth to her? As one marriage counselor puts it, "You cannot love a lie. You cannot love an image. You can love only the truth." A couple cannot enjoy a truly intimate marriage if one or the other is concealing a great lie or secret from the other. Authentic marriage is based on knowing and living and loving the truth—however painful it might be to reveal and to forgive.

The WWJD Strategy

In considering how to react to a painful revelation from your husband, perhaps the most important question to ask is, "What would Jesus do?" We find help with the answer to this question by reading the story from the gospel of John of the woman caught in the act of adultery:

> At dawn he appeared again in the temple courts, where all the people gathered around him, and he sat down to teach them. The teachers of the law and the Pharisees brought in a woman caught in adultery. They made her stand before the group and said to Jesus, "Teacher, this woman was caught in the act of adultery. In the Law Moses

commanded us to stone such women. Now what do you say?" They were using this question as a trap, in order to have a basis for accusing him.

But Jesus bent down and started to write on the ground with his finger. When they kept on questioning him, he straightened up and said to them, "Let any one of you who is without sin be the first to throw a stone at her." Again he stooped down and wrote on the ground.

At this, those who heard began to go away one at a time, the older ones first, until only Jesus was left, with the woman still standing there. Jesus straightened up and asked her, "Woman, where are they? Has no one condemned you?"

"No one, sir," she said.

"Then neither do I condemn you," Jesus declared. "Go now and leave your life of sin" (John 8:2-11).

What can a wife learn from this dramatic encounter? First, Jesus refuses to condemn a person willing to acknowledge their sin; second, he is willing to forgive even the most egregious sins; and third, he tells that person to leave their life of sin and to begin a new life going forward.

We cannot presume to tell you what you should ultimately do if your husband confesses to infidelity. Yet, if his motive is to truly repent of his past actions (meaning he will not do it again), clear his conscience, and restore integrity to his walk with God and you, it seems that offering him mercy and the opportunity to reconcile and rebuild trust is in keeping with the example of Jesus.

Here's something that may offer you encouragement. If your husband is willing to open up and talk to you about the most difficult secret his heart has ever had to bear, isn't it likely he will, going forward, be willing to tell you about everything else that's on his heart? If you choose to respond to his confession with grace and mercy, isn't the road now open for him to tell you anything and everything else about his life? Isn't such honesty and openness in your relationship what you have been wanting all along?

Life-Threatening Depression

What if my husband tells me he struggles with suicidal thoughts?

While this disclosure needs to be received with the utmost seriousness, we counsel against emotional overreaction or hysteria. That may serve only to keep him from sharing any further his ongoing struggles.

Experts in the field say there are as many as five different stages of suicidal contemplation, ranging from merely entertaining the possibility to actually determining to go through with it. Because neither we nor you are mental health experts, the only prudent thing to do is to take your husband seriously and seek professional help at once. But at the moment of his dark revelation, we urge a temperate and controlled response, such as:

> I am so grateful that you chose to share these painful thoughts with me. You must be living with some very agonizing emotions. I want you to know I will come alongside you in this struggle. I'm not qualified to say how serious your struggle with these thoughts truly is, but let's find someone who can tell us. Let's call our doctor and arrange an appointment today.

Should your husband object to calling someone, you should do so anyway—the obvious principle being it's better to be safe than sorry. If a health professional advises you to come in immediately for evaluation, but your husband objects or will not come with you, as a last resort you should call 911 and have him brought in for a twenty-four-hour evaluation at a local hospital emergency room.

If your husband has come to the point where he's willing to tell you about his inner battle with suicidal thoughts, it is clearly a cry for help and a warning sign of serious depression. If you have any reason to believe his struggle has progressed to the planning stage or worse, then physically stay with him until you have actually been seen by a professional and received their evaluation.

In summary, regardless of the difficult or even devastating news he reveals to you, it is vital you continue to show him the unconditional respect and nonjudgmental attitude he needs in order to keep the conversation going. Proverbs reminds us:

> One who has unreliable friends soon comes to ruin,
>> but there is a friend who sticks closer than a brother.
>> (Proverbs 18:24)

The Bible goes on to say one of the signs of true friendship is the freedom to share important matters openly:

> Perfume and incense bring joy to the heart,
>> and the pleasantness of a friend
>> springs from their heartfelt advice.
>> (Proverbs 27:9)

And yes, there are times when loving your friend means showing tough love:

> Wounds from a friend can be trusted,
>> but an enemy multiplies kisses.
>> (Proverbs 27:6)

Rebuilding a Trust Fund

Let's go on to address the issue of reconciliation and rebuilding trust. How can you know your husband, who has confessed something upsetting, is indeed willing to forsake his sin instead of justifying it to you? In Gary Chapman's very helpful book *The Five Languages of an Apology*, he refers to five *R*s: responsibility ("I did it"), remorse ("I'm sorry I did it"), repentance ("I won't do it again"), restitution ("I will make this right"), and a request ("Will you forgive me for doing it?").

If your spouse is sincere in his desire to reconcile with you, those five *R*s will be present. We often tell spouses that they can know their mate is sincere in their desire to forsake their sin if they start sounding like David sounded in Psalm 51:

For I know my transgressions,
 and my sin is always before me.
Against you, you only, have I sinned
 and done what is evil in your sight;
so you are right in your verdict
 and justified when you judge...
Cleanse me with hyssop, and I will be clean;
 wash me, and I will be whiter than snow...
Hide your face from my sins
 and blot out all my iniquity.
Create in me a pure heart, O God,
 and renew a steadfast spirit within me.
Do not cast me from your presence
 or take your Holy Spirit from me.
Restore to me the joy of your salvation
 and grant me a willing spirit, to sustain me.
    (Psalm 51:3-4,7,9-12)

Regardless of the painful or disturbing information your husband may share with you, if he does so in the spirit of David (and it will take time to confirm that is actually the case), you will eventually be convinced he is doing so to make things right rather than to break your heart.

Question 3: What if I lose my temper and get into an argument with my husband?

If you have been in the habit of responding quickly, and often with a tinge of anger, when your husband does share his thoughts, it will be difficult to change. The instinct to immediately fire back or express your disagreement or upset is likely based on some emotional pain that may linger in your heart.

Rebel with a Painful Cause

Jan had been raised in a home where her father physically abused her. His discipline involved punching his sons and daughters whenever he got upset. That deep inner scarring carried through to her adult-hood when she joined the military. Like many children of abuse, she developed hostility and a desire to control others as a fence to keep people away and from hurting her. As a result, Jan frequently got into arguments with her superiors, resulting in negative performance assessments.

Jan was still angry at her father—but she had generalized her rage toward all males and male officers in particular. She finally left the service a frustrated and sad person.

Jan's love life fared little better. She had trouble trusting a man and quickly found things that upset her about the men she dated. Eventually she would let loose and tell her current boyfriend everything about him that bothered her. While venting may have provided her temporary emotional relief, it usually led to the premature end of the relationship.

Hostile Territory for a Husband

If you as a wife can identify to a degree with Jan, and you have developed hostile and controlling instincts, letting your husband speak his mind may prove to be a monumental challenge. You have become so accustomed to defending yourself and protecting your heart with strong and even harsh words that it has become second nature. If that's the case, please hear the warning of Scripture:

> Sin is not ended by multiplying words,
> but the prudent hold their tongues.
> (Proverbs 10:19)

It's paradoxical behavior, but some women who verbally punish their husband are working to drive him away while at the same time longing for him to draw closer. They apparently believe the more they punish him with their words, the more he will see the error of his ways and snuggle up to her.

Unfortunately, most husbands, when wounded by the stinging words and hostile attitude of their wife, do just the opposite. They either respond in kind or choose to withdraw. Either way, the hurting wife is left alone feeling worthless and rejected—the very emotions that injured her heart deeply as a child.

There is a way to untie this Gordian knot. If you have used hostility and control as a means of protecting your wounded heart, recognize that your means of coping with life's problems has not served you well. If you set aside your angry and controlling behavior and instead listen with patience, acceptance, and sincerity to your husband, he will start talking to you. Once he starts talking to you, he will keep talking. Then the more he talks, the more of his heart he will reveal to you. The more he reveals his heart, the emotionally closer he will feel to you. The closer he feels to you, the more love he will begin displaying toward you.

You will likely receive at last, as the Bible puts it, "A good measure, pressed down, shaken together and running over, will be poured into your lap. For with the measure you use, it will be measured to you" (Luke 6:38). You may end up receiving what you longed for all along—the love of your husband.

If you do momentarily default to arguing or attacking, simply stop and apologize. There is never a better time to admit a wrong than just as soon as you have committed it:

> Fools mock at making amends for sin,
>> but goodwill is found among the upright.
>> (Proverbs 14:9)

Escaping the Trap

The Bible counsels a sense of urgency in admitting our mistake when we enter into a pledge we should not have made. Interestingly enough, this same advice works remarkably well for extricating us from situations where we have said hurtful or sinful things to others, including our spouse.

> My son, if you have put up security for your neighbor,
>> if you have shaken hands in pledge for a stranger,

you have been trapped by what you said,
> ensnared by the words of your mouth.
So do this, my son, to free yourself,
> since you have fallen into your neighbor's hands:
Go—to the point of exhaustion—
> and give your neighbor no rest!
Allow no sleep to your eyes,
> no slumber to your eyelids.
> > (Proverbs 6:1-4)

While it may take time to undo the damage done by arguing with your husband, the sooner you admit you were wrong and make amends, the sooner your relationship will get back on track. If your husband isn't used to you apologizing for your aggressive and hostile manner, a humble and heartfelt apology will make an impression on him. Over time he will come to believe something is changing with you. God may even use it to give him the encouragement to begin talking.

Engendering Verbal Abuse

Are you capable of verbal abuse toward your husband?

It's a myth that only men are verbally abusive; verbal abuse crosses gender lines. We knew one husband who had grown up in an environment where his mother frequently went into verbal tirades against her husband (often in front of her children). She would shout that she hated him, that people had warned her never to marry him, and on one occasion, that if she had a gun she would shoot him. This qualifies as verbal abuse by our standards.

If you have been verbally abusive toward your husband (or children), even mildly so, it is still a serious matter—it is sin. The Bible warns:

> The wise woman builds her house,
> > but with her own hands [and words] the foolish one tears
> > hers down.
> > > (Proverbs 14:1)

If you have been demolishing your house with your uncontrolled tongue, you need to admit the damage you have done and seek help. To not do so is to risk (at least emotionally) losing your husband and children. The book of James pulls no punches in describing the dangers of a tongue out of control:

> The tongue also is a fire, a world of evil among the parts of the body. It corrupts the whole body, sets the whole course of one's life on fire, and is itself set on fire by hell.
>
> All kinds of animals, birds, reptiles and sea creatures are being tamed and have been tamed by mankind, but no human being can tame the tongue. It is a restless evil, full of deadly poison (James 3:6-8).

Only One Remedy Available

Verbal abuse, while perhaps the product of being verbally abused yourself as a child, is also an act of our prideful human nature. There is only one remedy to such sin, and it is found in 1 John 1:6-9:

> If we claim to have fellowship with him and yet walk in the darkness, we lie and do not live out the truth. But if we walk in the light, as he is in the light, we have fellowship with one another, and the blood of Jesus, his Son, purifies us from all sin.
>
> If we claim to be without sin, we deceive ourselves and the truth is not in us. If we confess our sins, he is faithful and just and will forgive us our sins and purify us from all unrighteousness (1 John 1:6-9).

We must bring the sin of using our tongue for evil to the Lord Jesus for confession and cleansing. It is the blood of Jesus and his atoning death on the cross that alone can purify us from all sin, and that includes verbal abuse. To "walk in the light" means a willingness to openly confess our sin to God and to those we have harmed, seek their forgiveness, and allow God to restore our relationship. It is the simple formula that has fueled great spiritual revivals in the past.

Even when we sin, we have a Friend in heaven praying for us: "My dear children, I write this to you so that you will not sin. But if anybody does sin, we have an advocate with the Father—Jesus Christ, the Righteous One. He is the atoning sacrifice for our sins, and not only for ours but also for the sins of the whole world" (1 John 2:1-2).

The moment you lose your temper and say something harsh to your husband, imagine Jesus stepping up to the throne of God and, based on principles taught in the Word of God, saying something like this: "Heavenly Father, Mara has just spoken unkindly to her husband out of the pain and sin in her heart. Do not hold that against her for I have paid the penalty for her actions by my death on the cross. Send your Holy Spirit to convict her of what she has done so that she can be reconciled to you and to her husband. Heal her husband of the pain she has caused and heal her of her own hurts. She is your precious child, your eternal treasure, saved and redeemed by my blood."

Please remember, direction is destiny. If you are willing to change the way you react to your husband from hostility and control to patience and respect, it will change the destiny of your marriage. Even if your spouse does not change his behavior immediately, it will still have an impact on his life. We cannot promise he will instantly become the husband you have always longed for, but it will dramatically increase the chances of your marriage improving for the better.

Question 4: What if I'm afraid to get my husband to talk because when he does, he often blows up at me?

Sadly, this is a situation many wives face. They live in the constant tension or dread of saying something that will set their husband off. Knowing his hair-trigger temper, they are not only reluctant to get him to talk, they are frightened by the prospect. When he does start talking, it often ends with him controlling, shaming, punishing, and wounding their heart with his angry words.

If this is your situation, we are saddened by what you have suffered.

And we suggest here a short-term strategy and a long-term response for dealing with your verbally abusive husband. The goal is to get him to the place where he will talk to you in a pleasant, sincere, and respect-ful manner.

Drawing Needed Boundaries

Short-term, you must set clear and definite boundaries with your husband regarding his words and temper. But first a note of caution: if you believe setting and enforcing boundaries would cause him to escalate his verbal abuse or progress to even worse behavior, don't do it.

Instead, immediately seek professional help on your own from a Christian counselor or pastor and devise a plan to safeguard your phys-ical safety first and foremost. That may include asking your husband to leave the home while he receives help or you moving to a safe shelter for women. Again, never take the following short-term steps if you feel that doing so would endanger you in any way. A higher level of outside inter-vention is needed in your marriage than what these boundaries will pro-vide. For the sake of both of you and your marriage, seek that help now.

If rather than physical abuse the problem is your husband saying things he should not, then you need to address that issue one step at a time.

Step One is to inform him of a new boundary: "When you speak like this to me, it is damaging to me, our marriage, and to you. There-fore, I cannot continue this conversation unless you change your words and talk to me in a respectful manner." If he disregards this boundary and continues to say abusive things, then you move on to the next step.

Step Two is to enforce the new boundary. If he continues his verbal aggressiveness, say nothing further and leave the room. In most cases this will end the abuse for now. Few men are willing to go on arguing or shouting when they are the only one in the room.

However, if he follows you out of the room and continues the ver-bal abuse, it is necessary to exit the house. If he follows you when you exit the house, it would be wise for you to leave the neighborhood and go to some safe place. If he follows you as you leave the neighborhood, you should call the police. He needs to understand that he is account-able to others, not just to you, for how he treats you.

Step Three is to take advantage of the new boundary and seek help to uncover the issues in your husband's heart that produce this destructive behavior. The reason he has been insensitive or even harshly abusive with you is a combination of sin and pain. It is likely he was verbally abused growing up, and such mistreatment is the sad gift that keeps on giving from generation to generation—until it is confronted, resolved, and healed by the love and power of Christ.

An Abuser No More

Please remember there is hope for such husbands. The Scriptures are filled with examples of angry and verbally abusive men whose lives were changed by God. Paul the apostle was such a hostile man. He shares with his young protégé Timothy the story of the transformation of his life:

> I thank Christ Jesus our Lord, who has given me strength, that he considered me trustworthy, appointing me to his service. Even though I was once a blasphemer and a persecutor and a violent man, I was shown mercy because I acted in ignorance and unbelief. The grace of our Lord was poured out on me abundantly, along with the faith and love that are in Christ Jesus (1 Timothy 1:12-14).

That same man, who used to rage, blaspheme, and stand by while others (such as Stephen) were murdered, would later write what is called today "The Love Chapter" found in 1 Corinthians 13:

> Love is patient, love is kind. It does not envy, it does not boast, it is not proud. It does not dishonor others, it is not self-seeking, it is not easily angered, it keeps no record of wrongs. Love does not delight in evil but rejoices with the truth. It always protects, always trusts, always hopes, always perseveres (1 Corinthians 13:4-7).

It wouldn't be hard to live with a husband who spoke to you and treated you like the changed apostle Paul, would it? Paul gives this additional advice on how we should talk to one another:

Do not let any unwholesome talk come out of your mouths, but only what is helpful for building others up according to their needs, that it may benefit those who listen. And do not grieve the Holy Spirit of God, with whom you were sealed for the day of redemption. Get rid of all bitterness, rage and anger, brawling and slander, along with every form of malice. Be kind and compassionate to one another, forgiving each other, just as in Christ God forgave you (Ephesians 4:29-32).

The Abusive Christian—An Oxymoron

What of the husband who claims to be a Christian yet verbally abuses you and others? The Bible addresses such a contradiction:

With the tongue we praise our Lord and Father, and with it we curse human beings, who have been made in God's likeness. Out of the same mouth come praise and cursing. My brothers and sisters, this should not be. Can both fresh water and salt water flow from the same spring? My brothers and sisters, can a fig tree bear olives, or a grapevine bear figs? Neither can a salt spring produce fresh water (James 3:9-12).

The Bible is making a strong point. Our soul is either filled with fresh water or salt water; we are either a fig tree or a grapevine. We cannot be both. That is, for your husband to one moment profess his love for Jesus and the next moment shred your heart with his cruel words means either he is seriously out of fellowship with God or he is an unbeliever. The Bible addresses these two possibilities:

So I say, walk by the Spirit, and you will not gratify the desires of the flesh. For the flesh desires what is contrary to the Spirit, and the Spirit what is contrary to the flesh. They are in conflict with each other, so that you are not to do whatever you want. But if you are led by the Spirit, you are not under the law (Galatians 5:16-18).

174

It is possible to be a genuine follower of Jesus Christ and still allow the desires of our sinful nature to rule our actions (and our words). When that happens, this is what you can expect: "The acts of the flesh are obvious: sexual immorality, impurity and debauchery; idolatry and witchcraft; hatred, discord, jealousy, fits of rage, selfish ambition, dissensions, factions and envy; drunkenness, orgies, and the like" (Galatians 5:19-21).

If your husband is a true disciple of Christ, he will come under conviction that such behavior is contrary to the Holy Spirit's control in his life, and he will ultimately change course. However, if his verbally abusive behavior continues on and on, the Bible has an even more serious conclusion: "I warn you, as I did before, that those who live like this will not inherit the kingdom of God" (Galatians 5:21).

For him to continue living this way, only one possibility is left. Despite his claim that he is a Christian, sadly he is not. He needs to recognize that he is lost and in need of redemption and to ask Jesus to forgive him and give him the gift of eternal life: "This righteousness is given through faith in Jesus Christ to all who believe. There is no difference between Jew and Gentile, for all have sinned and fall short of the glory of God, and all are justified freely by his grace through the redemption that came by Christ Jesus" (Romans 3:22-24).

But if your husband is a Christian, yet he allows the sinful nature to control his emotions and tongue, is there hope for him to change? Yes, we have seen people face their pain and their sin and allow Christ to transform this part of their lives. God can change the heart and the speech of an abusive husband.

A Story of Healing and Change

Following a conference where we discussed wounded hearts, a couple asked us if they could tell us their story. Sean was raised in a home where his father made promises he rarely kept, and he eventually divorced Sean's mother. She was forced to work in order to support the family and was rarely home. From his earliest days Sean felt abandoned, both by his father who had left and his mother who was unavailable. As the oldest, he was under pressure to be the man of the house. As time went on, the hurt turned to pain, the pain to frustration, and the frustration to anger.

When he met Samantha, Sean found a soul mate who understood his pain. She too had grown up abandoned and alone. Her alcoholic mother left home while Samantha was still quite young, but she promised to visit her and the other kids frequently. So Samantha would stand at the window all dressed up waiting for her to arrive—only for her mother to never show up. She came to fear abandonment and to distrust relationships. Her progression of pain also landed her in a state of anger and depression.

After Sean and Samantha were married, it wasn't long until the arguments between them escalated. Simple frustrations and misunderstandings grew to screaming and shouting at each other. Sean felt unappreciated for how hard he tried to provide for the family. Samantha felt ignored and unloved by Sean's long hours at the office.

One evening the shouting match took an ominous turn—Sean pushed Samantha against the refrigerator door. She hit the door hard and was momentarily dazed. Then she ran into the bedroom and locked the door.

Sean left the house afraid and shaken by his actions. He knew he had gone too far and was the first to ask for help. They agreed to meet with their pastor and to separate for a season to work on their marriage.

During the weeks and months of pastoral care, they came to understand the damage done to their hearts as children. They realized each had core pain issues that caused them to step on each other's pain, often without realizing it. They were both Christians and knew they needed to forgive the people who had abandoned them.

Sean owned up to his verbal and physical abuse and acknowledged it for the terrible sin it was. As Samantha began to listen to Sean's story, she discovered many of the sources of his pain. Despite her own troubled past, she began to feel sorrow, empathy, and care for her husband's wounded heart. She began to understand how her angry words only further deepened his pain. She asked his forgiveness for not understanding how inadequate her words made him feel.

(Again, no excuses were made or allowed for Sean's violent actions—there is never any excuse for physically or verbally abusing another person. We always have other choices we can make when someone touches our core pain.)

As Sean listened to Samantha, he began to realize how his distant and detached behavior mimicked that of her mother. Sean's angry outbursts and self-focused actions would send Samantha deep into her rejection and abandonment pain. He realized he needed to offer her the assurance he would never leave her and to love her just as she is.

The pastor led them in prayer for Jesus to heal their hearts, and they began to experience redemptive grace. "We began to realize that we had options other than to escalate our arguments," Sean later said. "We could understand what the other person was truly asking for, which was love, respect, and acceptance."

It has been several years since that ugly incident in the kitchen that almost destroyed their marriage. Sean and Samantha and their one son now live together in peace. There has been no reoccurrence of domestic violence, and both continue to rejoice over the miracle God did in their marriage.

We share this story to underscore this truth: God can change a violent man into a person who is patient, accepting, and caring. He did that with the apostle Paul and he did that with Sean. He can do that in the life of your husband as well, but you will need to reach out for help rather than doing it alone.

Question 5: What if my husband has said he no longer loves me or that he's not interested in staying in the marriage?

It is always sad to receive a call or email from a wife whose husband has told her that he no longer loves her and wants out of the marriage. It is often accompanied by the news that he has a new girlfriend and is intending to marry or live with her once the divorce is final. It leaves the spouse with a sense of shock, disbelief, betrayal, and despair.

When things have progressed to this stage, is there any point in trying to get him to talk? Isn't it too late for that?

After the initial shock is over, a wife may start searching her own life to see if she caused this to happen. Perhaps she was too critical or distant or lacking in nurture or respect and drove him away. It's a characteristic of human nature to try and make sense out of things that make no sense—and the easiest explanation is to blame ourselves. Sadly, this only compounds the sorrow for the betrayed or jilted spouse. Not only has she lost her husband, but she is to blame for it—or so she tells herself. This is the wrong approach.

The Only Good Explanation

Leslie Vernick, a gifted Christian counselor and author, reminds her clients, often women who have been abused or abandoned or betrayed, that the only explanation for such cruel and unloving treatment is sin. The reason their spouse has betrayed his vows, entered into an affair with another person, and announced he no longer loves his wife is sin. Several verses in the Bible use the words *heart* and *wicked* in the same sentence. As the Bible bluntly reminds us,

> Haughty eyes and a proud heart—
>   the unplowed field of the wicked—produce sin.
> (Proverbs 21:4)

Or as the apostle Paul reminds us, "The acts of the flesh are obvious: sexual immorality, impurity and debauchery" (Galatians 5:19).

There Is Always Value in Honesty

So is there value in trying to get your husband to talk to you even if he has already decided to leave the marriage or seek a divorce? We believe it is always worthwhile to get someone to honestly and sincerely share their heart if they are willing. However, we can make no guarantees that your husband will change course as a result, and it's important to adjust your expectations.

There is always the possibility he will use the occasion to attack and blame you for his deceitful behavior. Husbands involved in infidelity can be so deep into their self-deception and self-focus that they are incapable of honestly sharing their heart. Until they undergo radical repentance, they will likely seek only to justify themselves and push you further away (typically out of guilt). If that turns out to be the case, there isn't any good purpose in continuing the discussion or letting him talk. He will only add to your pain and sorrow.

However, if he is willing to be truthful and open, then there is value in having that conversation. If he begins to talk, he may actually walk himself to the door of his core pain and see the reasons why he is pursuing the affair.

Infidelity as Self-Medication

If that happens, he may come to the startling realization that the reason he is leaving the marriage has little, if anything, to do with you. He may even realize that the pain that lured him into the affair will continue even after he leaves the marriage. We believe most affairs are the result of trying to deal with legitimate needs in an illegitimate way. Affairs, infidelities, and divorce are often self-medicating behaviors. Whether your husband realizes it or not, he has come to believe that the only solution for his soul-searing heart pain (which developed long before he ever met you) is the hormonal rush (what Gary Chapman calls the "tingles") he receives from infatuation and sexual involvement with his new girlfriend.

During this stage of the relationship, the sexual experiences are often intense, and the relationship is new and lacks any true responsibility. It is pleasure for pleasure's sake, and it causes the most detached of men to feel alive as never before (or at least not since their first honeymoon).

Such erring husbands naively believe that this new sexual high is the cure-all for the rejection, depression, inhibition, and detachment they have been dealing with all their life. If he does marry his new lover, it will take only a few months for him to realize that all the inner pain that shut him down emotionally in his first marriage is still at work. Only now he has a bigger mess on his hands with the relational chaos of the divorce, the escalated financial obligations of the settlement, and the unintended consequence of kids who don't want to speak to him.

Because an affair rarely resolves the pain in someone's heart, the divorce percentages for second marriages are even higher than for first marriages (by about 26 percent, according to some studies). The numbers for third marriages are even more distressing. Approximately 90 percent of third marriages end in divorce. If finding a new lover and engaging in euphoric sexual thrills could heal the human heart, then second and third marriages should have a higher success rate than first marriages. That's not reality.

Help His Heart Come to Freedom

So what value is there in getting a straying husband to talk? Your first goal has to be to help him start down the road toward freedom from pain in his heart (which we'll explain in a moment), not to rescue the marriage. If you insist that saving the marriage is your first priority, and he has already decided he doesn't want to rescue the marriage, the end result will be he won't talk to you.

But many husbands, even erring ones, can be persuaded to talk if you ask them the right question. What is that question? Our good friend John Regier often poses this question to men reluctant to seek help: "How much longer do you wish to live with the pain in your heart?" Few men ever respond, "Oh, I like this pain I feel. I'm willing to live with it for several more decades." No, most respond, "You mean I could get rid of this? How?"

If you can get your husband to talk, he may be able to identify the pain he has carried in his heart most of his life. Once he has identified it, he may be open to pastoral care to help him find freedom from it. If that pain and sin can be resolved and he comes to freedom, he will be able to emotionally connect his heart to yours. Once that happens, his desire for a divorce usually fades away. His need to self-medicate by using a new lover usually vanishes with it. We have seen such changes take place in the hearts of men who were involved in an emotional or physical affair and chose to return to their marriage.

Is it possible that, as his wife, you have been stepping on his pain without knowing it? It happens all the time. That's how the husband comes to associate his pain with your presence in his life (and thus his logic that a new lover or wife would take away that pain).

The Setup for an Affair

Again, we want to be careful to assert that your behavior in no way justifies his adulterous behavior. There are always infinitely far better options for dealing with pain than breaking one's wedding vows. It just may be that you will learn that some of your behaviors or attitudes have unfortunately contributed to his conclusion that the marriage is not working for him, nor will it ever work.

How does that happen? Some wives who are overly expressive (they do all the talking) or critical (they are always correcting or judging) or controlling (they are always right and insist on the last word) may help create the condition wherein hurting (often emotionally submissive) and lonely (often quiet and inhibited) and despairing (often rejected and impulsive) husbands can come to believe there is no way out of their pain except to find another woman.

This does not justify the husband's adultery (again, we always have options that don't involve sin for what to do with our pain), but it may have helped create an environment ripe for an affair.

We did a radio interview one day on "getting your husband to talk." We discussed some of the principles in this book, such as the importance of playing catch instead of ping-pong when talking with your husband. A woman caller came on the line and said, "Oh, my, I have done everything wrong. I pushed my husband to talk to me. I demanded that he answer me. I criticized him for his lack of response. I argued with him when he did answer me. I've done everything wrong and now we are separated. I'm going to change. I'm going to begin asking him questions and let him answer. I'm going to listen before I begin telling him what I think. Please pray for me that it's not too late."

Rather than being offended by the suggestion that she had contributed to her husband's shutting down, this caller sounded genuinely grateful to learn that even though she had made some mistakes, perhaps it was not too late to fix them. We couldn't help but believe that her humility and openness to change offered real hope for this couple to reconcile.

A Final Attempt to Reach His Heart

If your husband has left or announced his intention to divorce, we suggest you write him a letter and say something similar to this (restated in your own words):

> I realize that you have made up your mind this marriage is over. You have concluded that your only course of action is to leave and find someone else who will make you happier. Even if that is how things turn out, I would like to say this to you before you leave.
>
> I now realize that both of us brought heart damage due to sin and pain to this marriage. We both grew up experiencing unwanted hurts that limited or shut down our ability to give and receive love. We made some wrong choices in response to our pain. When we met each other, we didn't really understand the heart damage we were bringing to our relationship. The infatuation and strong attraction we felt for each other covered over that pain. Our emotions convinced us that we had met the person who could make us happy for a lifetime.
>
> We both know that's not how things worked out. Whether we meant to or not, we began to step on each other's pain. Each time we did that we put one more brick on the wall we were building in our hearts to block out each other. Eventually we came to the point where we couldn't give and receive love the way we needed to. The inner pain we felt caused us both to become self-focused.
>
> A sense of sadness, even despair set in. We began to look for ways to self-medicate our hearts. Perhaps I did that by throwing myself into raising the children or developing my friendships, and perhaps you did that by giving yourself to your work or sports or whatever.

Obviously, the day came when the pain in your heart grew so bad you decided you couldn't take it any longer. That opened you up to the possibility of finding someone else. To make matters worse, during all the years we were hurting inside, we weren't very good at listening to each other. I may have rarely given you the opportunity to say what was in your heart without criticizing you, telling you my opinion, or pointing out where you were wrong. I never wanted to shut you down, but I fear that I did, and I apologize for that. Sin allowed pride to block our communication for both of us.

Even if you still choose to end our marriage, I want to be able to say before that happens that for once I stopped to genuinely listen to your heart. Because we have children, we will be forced to have continued contact with each other. It's vital that they not see their parents angry and despising each other—they will have enough hurt already to deal with, and we don't want to add to it.

So if you're willing, I'd like the opportunity to meet with you just to listen, perhaps with a pastor or counselor present. My promise is that I won't interrupt you, I won't argue with you, I won't try to fix you—I only want to understand and care about what's in your heart. I'll listen as long as you wish to talk. If we don't have time to finish, we can meet again. I want to do now what I should have done when we first began our relationship.

Regardless of our future, I don't want you to continue carrying the pain in your heart for the rest of your life. If by letting you talk and listening to you I can help release some of that pain, or at least care about it going forward, I'd like to do that. Would you be willing to get together so I can just listen?

While there are no guarantees that your husband will say yes to such an offer, you have little to lose in making it. It's a calculated risk, but it could possibly yield a breakthrough. Even if he says no, you can have the peace of mind that you tried to do the right thing.

What if he says yes? By meeting with him and letting him talk, you may begin to experience an emotional breakthrough in your relationship. The natural next step would be to continue meeting with a pastor or counselor who could help move you toward reconciliation.

At the same time, we recommend you access the excellent seminars on DVD and CD available from Caring for the Heart Ministries in Colorado Springs, Colorado. In particular we encourage you to listen to the seminars "Rekindling Marital Intimacy" and "Caring for the Emotionally Damaged Heart." These resources and more are available online at caringfortheheart.com. Click on "Counseling Resources" and follow the directions from there. You may also wish to order CDs of our marriage conference, "For Better, For Worse, For Keeps," available at www.forkeepsministries.com under "Products."

Question 6: What if I've tried everything you've suggested and my husband still won't talk?

We hope we've been honest enough with you to admit that there are no foolproof methods or fail-safe techniques guaranteed to get your husband to talk. All you can do is pray and then try to create the right conditions for him to talk. The decision of whether he will do so still belongs to him. If after your best attempts he still will not talk to you, we suggest the following options:

Option 1: Ask a trusted friend to talk to your husband.

Sometimes a man will open up to another man even though he is reluctant to talk to his wife. There can be a variety of reasons for this, usually owing to past negative experiences. The story in the introduction is a case in point—Dan would not talk to Joan because of her past critical and angry responses to him. When Joan asked Bob to meet with Dan, Bob received an entirely different response. Dan talked for an entire hour nearly without taking a breath.

As a first step, it may be necessary to have another man invite your husband to lunch or a game or some other activity so that the friend can begin listening to your husband. As he begins to talk and open up, it may be possible for that friend to encourage your husband to begin talking to you.

Perhaps it goes without saying, but if you want your husband to talk as openly with you as he did with another man, then you need to listen to him in the same manner the other man did—with a respectful, nonjudgmental attitude and a sincere desire to care about the issues in his heart. As the Bible reminds us,

> The purposes of a person's heart are deep waters,
>> but one who has insight draws them out.
>> (Proverbs 20:5)

Option 2: Have someone invite your husband to join a men's small group or Bible study.

This is a variation on the first suggestion. Rather than encouraging your husband to speak to a specific person, you encourage him to seek out a small group where he could feel comfortable sharing his heart. Men's Bible studies or small groups are an excellent place for a man to start feeling accepted and understood.

Why is it important he bond with other men? Studies show that most men do not have one close friend. This has been true for decades in our society. With such self-imposed isolation comes loneliness, and with loneliness desperation, and with desperation comes undesirable behavior. Men who have no close friends to share their struggles with can be easy prey for our adversary. The Bible warns us, "Be alert and of sober mind. Your enemy the devil prowls around like a roaring lion looking for someone to devour" (1 Peter 5:8). On the positive side, the Bible tells us men benefit from having other friends in their lives:

> As iron sharpens iron,
>> so one person sharpens another.
>> (Proverbs 27:17)

As your husband begins to share his daily struggles, temptations, and hurts with other sympathetic men, healing, wisdom, and new strength may begin to develop in his heart.

How will this help your marriage? Once your husband sees and experiences the value of talking with other men, he may one day be ready to take the next step and begin talking to you. At the risk of being redundant, if you wish for your husband to talk to you the way he talks to the men in his group, you will need to respond to him the way other men do—with patience, acceptance, and sincerity.

Option 3: Observe the people he opens up to and ask them later how they do it.

Even if your husband is not ready to freely share his thoughts with you, there are likely other people in his life that he does open up to. The key is to watch for situations where he does talk freely to someone. Make mental notes on what the other person does to effectively draw him into the conversation.

Here is a quick sum of principles we have observed that can cause an otherwise quiet man to start talking:

Ask a man about a subject he enjoys and then just listen. One of our friends loves to travel by air. While otherwise given to sitting quietly, if someone asks him about his most recent plane trip, he quickly sits up and begins to talk. If the other person asks detailed questions about the type of aircraft he flew on, this man is soon using his hands to explain the various turns and maneuvers the plane could make.

If you ask meaningful follow-up questions, you will motivate a man to continue talking. You don't have to be an expert to ask good follow-up questions, just sincerely interested. Asking questions that clarify or call for more information is the equivalent of waving the green flag at a NASCAR race. It signifies to the driver that the track is clear and the race is on full speed. Asking a man good follow-up questions gives him the emotional fuel to keep talking, which is what you want to happen.

If you are unconditionally respectful and affirming, a man will keep talking. As we watched the people who could get men to talk, we noted that what they did not say was as important as what they did say. They never said anything critical, condemning, or condescending. Rather, they would just smile, nod, and express admiration for what the otherwise quiet men were telling them.

Finally, if you are willing to sit and listen as long as a man is willing to talk, he will keep talking. It's obvious to most of us when someone is giving us their polite attention but they intend to move on as soon as they can. It's also clear to us when someone settles in, looks us in the eye, and communicates with their body language they are here to stay.

Which of these people do you think the quiet male is going to open up to? Remember, many quiet men have never been listened to. They just assume that anyone they meet isn't interested in what they have to say or doesn't have the time. That's why people who get others to talk usually sit down and give the other person their full and undivided attention. They aren't constantly checking their phone for text messages or scanning the room to decide who might be more interesting to talk to.

Regardless of how quiet or isolated your husband may act with you, there is likely at least one person (or more) that he does talk to. It may be the guy behind the counter at the hardware store, the usher at church who welcomes him, or the nephew who comes to visit. Once you observe your husband come to life and start talking to other people, take careful note—that person is doing several things that you can learn to imitate.

Option 4: Plan enjoyable, nonpressurized activities (that both of you enjoy) where you can be together for long and unhurried periods of time.

One of Bob's happier memories from his high school years is going to professional football games with his father. While his father was quiet and sometimes withdrawn at home, seated in the end zone of a football stadium on a chilly December day, he would come alive. He would laugh, cheer, and occasionally stand up and shout with other fans seated nearby. Bob's dad once coached football in high school, so he loved the game. Both before and after the games, father and son would discuss the team, the coach, and various players.

This illustrates a principle that applies to many quiet men: put them in an enjoyable, nonpressurized activity for an extended period of time, and they will begin to talk.

It may be that you need to take the sacrificial step of going to sporting events with your husband even if you don't enjoy the game. If he is enjoying himself, chances are he will share that excitement with you and that could be the start of getting him to talk.

Perhaps you need to go hunting or on a fishing expedition with him. Again, you don't have to enjoying shooting game or cleaning slimy fish, but it will give you two extended time together. He will appreciate your companionship more than he can say.

Maybe your husband is drawn to things like computers and technology. Go to a nearby computer store and sit through a seminar with him. Or look for a trade show coming to your area and buy tickets for the two of you to go to that. Maybe he loves certain foods or outdoor barbecuing. Bob loves barbecue in almost any form and jumps at the chance to go with Cheryl to any place known for good brisket and sweet coleslaw.

What about joining your husband when he's cleaning the garage or raking up leaves in the fall? As we've said before, men will talk when they're doing an activity. If you're the person doing that activity with him, guess who he's going to talk to.

Option 5: Ask him if he will go with you to get help solving pain issues in your life, not his.

Many men see going to a counselor as the equivalent of a visit to the dentist for a root canal (or maybe two at once). But if you ask him to accompany you to a counselor for his input to solve *your* pain issues, he may be open to the idea. Be sure to seek out a biblical counselor or gifted pastor. It is just the better part of wisdom. Perhaps you could introduce the idea like this:

> I realize I have a number of heart issues I brought to our marriage. Some have hurt you. These pain issues grew out of things that happened to me even before we met. There's no one on earth who knows me as well as you do. Would

you be willing to come along as I work on my problems? You have a perspective on my life no one else does. The counselor may want to ask you questions about me that only you can answer.

You must be sincere rather than use this approach as a ploy. That is, even if your husband never opens up in these sessions about his own issues, you need to be okay with that. You are there to find help for you—not for him—and your husband can play an important role in offering his insights and observations from years of living with you.

If he is unwilling to go with you, go by yourself. If all that comes from your seeking help is that you experience freedom in your own heart, won't it have been well worth the effort? And if your husband is willing to accompany you during these sessions, he will have the opportunity to share his insights about you with the counselor—in other words, he will start talking. This could lead to the day when he begins to open up and talk with you, not only about your issues but also about pain in his own life. This is particularly likely if he sees that the pastoral care has had a positive impact on your life and the marriage.

The focus at this point is you leading by example in seeking help.

Option 6: Pray and fast for an opening to care about your husband's heart.

While we have saved this suggestion for last, it is actually the first thing a wife should do. There is no more powerful force on earth to change people or the course of events than prayer and fasting. *Prayer* is simply communicating your need with the heart of Jesus. *Fasting* is focused prayer that foregoes eating and normal pleasures to urgently call on God to answer.

This call to prayer and fasting is emphasized by Paul in the context of the spiritual warfare we encounter in our lives: "And pray in the Spirit on all occasions with all kinds of prayers and requests" (Ephesians 6:18).

Sometimes the struggle to get your husband to talk is at heart a spiritual issue. If your husband has become quiet and withdrawn due to past deep trauma, spiritual strongholds of fear, bitterness, or despair may be at work in his life. That doesn't mean he's under the control of the devil; it means simply that overwhelming pain has opened the door to spiritual oppression.

If this is the case, it's vital that you and others wrestle in prayer on his behalf. You might pray, *Dear Lord, we bind the powers that are binding my husband's heart. We ask in the victorious name of Jesus that you set him free from this and allow him to become all you created him to be. Amen.*

It's important to not overspiritualize issues that are otherwise emotional or relational problems or say to your husband, "The devil has you in his grip. That's why you won't talk to me." That will do far more lasting damage than good.

Yet, to read the Bible in its clear and plainspoken sense is to discover that there are times when our battle is not simply against "flesh and blood," as Paul states:

> Finally, be strong in the Lord and in his mighty power. Put on the full armor of God, so that you can take your stand against the devil's schemes. For our struggle is not against flesh and blood, but against the rulers, against the authorities, against the powers of this dark world and against the spiritual forces of evil in the heavenly realms (Ephesians 6:10-12).

Bill had lived in the grip of alcoholism his entire marriage, and he called our television program and eventually told us this story. When he and his brother were nine and eleven, their dad sent them into the woods to cut firewood for the family. The father handed the boys a chainsaw and told them not to come back until they had a load of wood for the stove. The boys walked deep into the woods and began cutting up fallen trees.

Without warning, the chainsaw jumped (as they will when they hit knotholes) and severely cut the older brother's leg. Bill, unable to staunch the bleeding, tried to drag his brother to help. By the time he reached home, it was too late—his brother had bled to death. That event shattered the young boy's heart. He shut down inside and eventually turned to alcohol for relief.

Sadly, we face an enemy so cruel that he will use a childhood accident to put the heart of a nine-year-old boy in bondage for a lifetime. Only prayer and fasting, turning in faith to the forgiveness and healing of the gospel of Jesus Christ and standing in the power of his name, can break such a stronghold.

One veteran of the Middle East wars was unable to open his heart to his wife. He had witnessed a mortar explosion that killed several of his friends. He came home with a wall of grief, trauma, and survivor guilt that caused him to quit talking. His wife prayed earnestly that he would seek help, and he did. Today he is a changed man, and his marriage is the primary recipient of his spiritual and emotional healing.

God answers prayer.

If your husband has quit talking, and other explanations and remedies have failed to set him free, he may be facing a spiritual battle, not simply an emotional one. You and others need to intercede for your husband for God to help bring his heart to freedom.

In the New Testament, Jesus miraculously gave voice to men who were literally unable to speak: "Great crowds came to him, bringing the lame, the blind, the crippled, the mute and many others, and laid them at his feet; and he healed them" (Matthew 15:30).

While your husband may be able to physically speak, spiritual and emotional issues may be keeping him from speaking his heart. Praise God our Lord Jesus can heal such a man and set him free from years of frustration, loneliness, and inner pain. The starting place to such freedom is calling on the Lord in prayer.

Even Paul asked his friends to pray that God would give him the ability to speak what was in his heart: "Pray also for me, that whenever I speak, words may be given me so that I will fearlessly make known the mystery of the gospel, for which I am an ambassador in chains. Pray that I may declare it fearlessly, as I should" (Ephesians 6:19-20).

It is not wrong to ask in prayer, *Lord Jesus, please work in my husband so that he might be able to speak what is in his heart without fear or anxiety and come to freedom. Amen.*

Conclusion

We've looked at several of the most common questions wives have in getting their husband to talk. While this chapter is by no means exhaustive, we hope it encourages you to believe that there are other answers and options to try even when it appears you have hit a dead end.

We have seen a principle at work in marriage that can help you regardless of the issues you face: *husbands are drawn to wives who listen; wives are drawn to husbands who talk.* If you begin to put this principle into practice by listening to your husband, you may see him reciprocate, and your marriage will begin a new and fulfilling chapter.

Questions to Consider

1. Which of you is the more talkative person and which is the quiet one in your marriage? If you are the quiet person, what would it mean to you for your husband to listen to you more? What advice did the elderly Eli give to his young servant, Samuel, in 1 Samuel 3:9? Is this something that can apply to all of us?

2. Why is there a risk in learning all the hidden issues in your husband's heart? Why is it important to decide beforehand how you will react if your husband should tell you something upsetting or even potentially devastating? What help is Proverbs 29:11 in preparing our hearts to hear such unsettling disclosures? What are some practical ways to keep your emotions under control?

3. Have you lost your temper in the past when talking to your husband? What was the practical impact of that on his willingness to talk to you? What are the elements of a sincere apology?

4. If you were to honestly evaluate how your husband talks to you, which of the following words characterize him? Is he

respectful, patient, indifferent, impatient, angry, or abusive? If your husband is verbally abusive, why is it critically important that you seek outside help now? What is keeping you from doing that? According to James 1:19-20, does anything good ever come from sinful anger?

5. What impact does building a wall of sin and pain in our hearts have on extinguishing feelings of love? According to Revelation 2:4-5, can we lose our first love for God? Can we lose it for one another? What remedy does Scripture suggest? How could letting your husband talk begin the process of restoring your first love?

6. How does the promise found in Ephesians 3:20-21 apply to your marriage? Are you willing to ask for outside help if you have come to a dead end? Where would be the best place to begin in finding such help? What is keeping you from doing that today?

Conclusion

How important is it to a couple's future for the wife to get her husband to talk?

When Alberto and Sonia sat down at our desk, despair and dejection were written all over their faces. Both seemed to share little hope that their marriage of seven years could be rescued. Sonia had discovered that Alberto was tweeting a girlfriend from high school, and that revelation had sent their marriage to the brink.

As we began to listen to their story, we learned that Alberto's sister had been killed in a car accident when Alberto was in elementary school. He had been very close to his sister and her death devastated him. What was just as devastating was that no one in Alberto's family had comforted him during this tragedy. He was forced to sit through the wake and funeral all on his own.

Sonia knew that Alberto had lost his sister, but she had never heard that no one—no one—had offered him any compassion and comfort in the days that followed her tragic death. You could see her heart soften toward her husband as she listened to and contemplated the emotional damage he endured. She began to wonder how she would have survived such a trauma of neglect had it been her sister who died.

As the week wore on, she began to move closer to Alberto. Day after day she began to understand and care about the immense grief and pain he had carried in his heart most of his life.

On the last day of our meeting together, God gave us the verse, "My Father's house has many rooms; if that were not so, would I have told you that I am going there to prepare a place for you? And if I go and prepare a place for you, I will come back and take you to be with me that you also may be where I am" (John 14:2-3).

The idea that God had prepared a room in his house for Alberto's sister and that someday Alberto could be reunited with her led to a fountain of tears and cleansing weeping on his part. Sonia instinctively reached over and held her husband in her arms as he shed the tears he should have wept at his sister's funeral so many decades ago.

When Alberto was finished with his weeping, he looked up, and his eyes glistened with light. Sonia could immediately see the difference. Something had changed inside her husband and the transformation radiated in his countenance.

Months later, Sonia contacted us to say she had a new husband. She and Alberto had fallen in love all over again. They had now become nearly inseparable.

How important is it for a wife to get her husband to talk?

Just ask Alberto and Sonia. They say they are still on their second honeymoon.

Appendix

A Personal Heart Examination

In order to help you assess your openness and ability to listen to your husband, we have included this Personal Heart Exam. The Personal Heart Exam helps identify areas of pain and sin where you may have hardened your heart, the place where you give and receive love.

A hardened or damaged or locked heart will cause you to react rather than respond to your spouse, and it builds barriers in your ability to give love to and receive love from your husband. Both of you may wish to take this test separately to determine what issues could be emotionally and spiritually at work in your relationship. Suggested prayers are offered at the end of each section of the test to help you begin resolving these pain and sin issues.

For a more complete discussion of resolving heart issues, we suggest you read our book, *The Marriage Miracle: How Soft Hearts Can Make a Couple Strong* (Harvest House Publishers, 2010).

Section A

Circle any of the following statements that are true about you or your parents (or your stepparents if they had a major influence on you growing up) if the statement is true some or most of the time. Otherwise, leave the number uncircled. Instructions for the self-scoring key are found at the end of the exam.

1. I grew up often feeling I was all on my own.

2. I was raised by parents who were too busy to notice me.

3. I was often upset or frightened by my father's or mother's temper.

4. I remember being sexually abused by someone when I was growing up.

5. My father or mother would simply shut down their emotions and feel nothing.

6. I was criticized for not measuring up to my father's or mother's standards.

7. I grew up in an environment where people rarely said, "I forgive you."

8. My father or mother always had to have the last word in any conversation.

9. When one of my parents got depressed, they would ignore or neglect the rest of us.

10. My mother or father would get upset when someone told them what to do.

11. I discovered pornography kept in our house.

12. I was taught that a career or earning money is the true measure of success.

13. I never felt I was good enough no matter how hard I tried.

14. When I was hurting, no one reached out to comfort me.

15. I was sometimes spanked too hard or slapped in anger.

16. My dad or mother could easily get emotionally upset.

17. I always felt I was a disappointment to my parents.

18. When I was young, I was left alone for hours to take care of myself.

19. It seemed like money was the one thing that made my parents happy.

20. My father would watch movies with explicit sexual scenes.

21. I grew up being taught to distrust those in authority.

22. My mother or father would go to a room and not come out if they were sad or upset.

23. One of my parents was overly controlling.

24. Old hurts and wounds caused by others were often rehearsed at our dinner table.

25. Our family was happy when we had money and miserable when we were broke.

26. One of my parents had an affair while I was growing up.

27. One of my parents wanted little or nothing to do with God.

28. I was afraid of making a mistake because of the rejection I would experience.

29. One parent would just walk away if the other parent started to argue with them.

30. I was sometimes slapped, hit with a fist, or beaten with a belt as a form of discipline.

31. I had to emotionally prop up one of my parents when they were sad or depressed.

32. My father or mother would get very upset if they did not get their way.

33. I rarely heard the words "I forgive you" growing up.

34. One of my parents often swore or used profanity.

35. My parents would make promises to me, and then just forget about them.

36. My father or mother abandoned our home when I was young.

37. I sometimes fear I'm going to end up in life all alone.

38. I sometimes think I could just disappear and no one would care.

39. I sometimes find myself swearing under my breath.

40. The memories of abuse in my home are just too painful to talk about.

41. When someone mistreats me, I can disconnect and not feel anything.

42. I have to do everything just right in life to feel good about myself.

43. I think people should earn my forgiveness if they've hurt me.

44. I need to feel in charge to feel comfortable.

45. I can't focus on the needs of others when I'm really sad or down.

46. I really don't like having a boss I have to report to; I'd rather work for myself.

47. I spend a good deal of time each day thinking about sexual fantasies.

48. I'll put in long overtime hours at work if I can gain recognition for it.

49. I'm depressed when other people are able to buy nice things I can't afford.

50. I enjoy reading racy romance novels or watching steamy movies.

51. I resent people telling me what to do.

52. I tend to think only about my own problem(s) until they are resolved.

53. I enjoy telling others what to do; it's the way to get something done.

54. People who mistreat you should pay the price for it.

55. Most people are lazy; they do just enough to get by.

56. I have a hard time remembering large periods of my life.

57. Someone used sex to hurt me when I was younger.

58. I have gotten into real trouble for losing my temper.

59. If I don't take care of myself, no one else will.

60. I fear the people that I love will one day leave me.

61. I find it hard to sympathize with people who are hurting.

62. I try to help people by pointing out their weaknesses or shortcomings.

63. I feel like damaged goods.

64. I often regret things I've said in an argument.

65. I frequently forget important things like anniversaries or birthdays.

66. I worry that someday I will be all alone.

67. Making a good living is my number one goal in life.

68. I have a sexual fantasy life no one knows anything about.

69. I don't like anyone telling me what to do.

70. I forget about the needs of others when I'm depressed.

71. I've been told I come on too strong with other people.

72. I've been told I have a hard time forgiving others.

73. I've been told I'm too married to my work.

74. I've been told I overreact when someone tells me to do something.

75. I've been told I tend to dominate people.

76. I've been told I'm a perfectionist.

77. I've been told I don't know how to enjoy life.

78. I've been told I'm too sensitive to criticism.

79. I've been told I have a lust problem.

80. I've been told I just check out when things get too intense.

81. I've been told I have trouble asking for forgiveness.

82. I've been told others worry how often I get depressed.

83. I've been told I have a problem with my temper.

84. I've been told I worry too much about being all alone in life.

Section B

Please circle the number if the statement is true of your personal thoughts or behavior some or most of the time. If it is not, leave it uncircled. Instructions for the self-scoring key are found at the end of the exam.

1. I struggle with evil thoughts toward others.

2. I find myself attracted to movies that include sexual immorality.

3. I take things from others but don't return them.

4. I sometimes wish a person who has hurt me would suffer or even die.

5. I sometimes look at others with lustful thoughts.

6. I find myself always wanting more than what I already own.

7. I can carry a deep grudge for an extended period of time.

8. I will tell a small lie to avoid getting into trouble.

9. I sometimes enjoy hearing dirty jokes.

10. I can be jealous of someone else's looks or accomplishments.

11. I like to think I know more than most people.

12. I will say bad things about other people behind their back.

13. I have made foolish decisions I later regretted.

14. I disregard the warnings of others if I think I know better.

15. I like to be the one person everyone notices in a room.

16. I can say harsh or biting things about other people.

17. I'm sad or upset when other people get recognized and I don't.

18. I sometimes linger rather than turn away when illicit scenes occur in a movie.

19. I sometimes lie when it's just as easy to tell the truth.

20. I hope something bad happens to my enemies.

21. No matter how much money I have, I always seem to want more.

22. I flirt with someone else's spouse now and then.

23. I get so angry at others that I want to hurt them.

24. I sometimes fudge a little on taxes or financial reports.

25. I was involved in premarital sexual experiences.

26. I sometimes imagine myself doing things that I know are wrong.

27. I struggle with feelings of hatred toward someone.

28. I take things from work and don't return them.

29. I enjoy making eye contact with an attractive person even if they're married.

30. I struggle with resentment.

31. I find obscene jokes amusing.

32. Occasionally I will spread damaging information about other people.

33. I don't like consulting with others before making a big decision.

34. I dwell on sexual experiences I had outside of marriage.

35. I have to admit there are some people I almost hate.

36. I am attracted to owning nice things in order to impress others.

37. I sometimes put on appearances.

38. I get upset when someone else gets something I really wanted.

39. I associate with certain people just to make me look good.

40. I sometimes have hateful thoughts about other people.

41. I will watch a sexually explicit program when no one else is looking.

42. I borrow things from others and don't tell them I did.

43. I can get so upset with someone that I hope they will die sooner than expected.

44. I find myself fantasizing about others during married sexual intimacy.

45. I am willing to put others in second place to get ahead in life.

46. I have some feelings of ill will toward others.

47. I sometimes tell little white lies.

48. I sometimes think about sensual images from the Internet or movies during married intimacy.

49. I am jealous of others I perceive to be just above my level.

50. I sometimes share confidential or embarrassing things about others.

51. I know I can handle life on my own.

52. I get a thrill from taking risky chances with my money.

53. I have deep grievances I continue to carry.

54. Buying things makes me happy, but soon I'm wishing I had something else.

55. I think a lot about my former boyfriend or girlfriend even though I'm married.

56. I can't help hating certain people who have treated me badly.

57. I borrow things from others but can take months (or years) to return them.

58. I give a second glance to a sexy person who passes by.

59. I know some of my thoughts are wrong—but I can't stop thinking them.

60. I am a thrill-seeker who enjoys taking chances.

61. I feel I'm usually right and others are usually wrong.

62. I will sometimes say or hint at things that could damage someone else's reputation.

63. I resent it when I am passed over in favor of someone else.

64. I will listen to a dirty joke now and then.

65. I exaggerate to make me sound better or more impressive than I am.

66. I spend too much time daydreaming about sexual fantasies.

67. I take things without asking.

68. I dwell on how people I dislike should suffer for their sins.

69. I can despise a person who mistreats me.

70. I can look at other people, even if they are married, and wish I were in a romantic relationship with them.

71. I can use spiteful words talking about others.

72. I make quick and impulsive decisions.

73. I like to read the details about celebrities who get caught in a sexual scandal.

74. I will punish others with the silent treatment.

75. I push myself to always earn more than I did last year.

76. I don't mind when I leave people with a false impression of what I'm thinking.

77. I wish I could live someone else's life rather than my own.

78. I know more about living life than most people I know.

Personal Heart Examination Scoring Key

Using the answer sheets from the Personal Heart Exam, Section A, circle each number below that you circled in the exam. Then count the number of times you circled a number on each line and put the total at the end of that line under Score.

Section A: The Types of a Hardened Heart

								Score
Abandoned Heart	1	14	35	37	60	66	84	_____
Rejected Heart	2	13	33	38	59	65	78	_____
Angry Heart	3	16	34	39	58	64	83	_____
Defiled Heart	4	15	30	40	57	63	77	_____
Detached Heart	5	18	29	41	56	61	80	_____
Judgmental Heart	6	17	28	42	55	62	76	_____
Bitter Heart	7	24	36	43	54	72	81	_____
Controlling Heart	8	23	32	44	53	71	75	_____
Proud Heart	9	22	31	45	52	70	82	_____
Rebellious Heart	10	21	27	46	51	69	74	_____
Immoral Heart	11	20	26	47	50	68	79	_____
Temporal Heart	12	19	25	48	49	67	73	_____

Taking the Next Steps

Now that you've completed the questions in Section A and totaled the score for each type of hardened or locked heart, look for your scores that have the highest number. A score of zero means you do not struggle with this type of locked heart. A score of one to two indicates it may be a slight problem. A score of three to five suggests this is an important issue in your life. A score of six to seven indicates you likely have a serious heart issue in this area. It's common to have one or more types of locked heart in your life. Taking your list of hardened hearts, starting with the highest scores first, pray through each hardened heart using the following prayer:

> *Dear Lord Jesus, I confess that I struggle with a* [name the type of hardened heart] *that is the result of my painful experiences and sinful choices. I ask your forgiveness for my hardened heart and choose to renounce a* [name the type of hardened heart]. *I ask you to remove it from my life and in its place to give me a softened heart.*
>
> *I claim the Bible's promise of Ezekiel 36:26, "I will give you a new heart and put a new spirit in you; I will remove from you your heart of stone and give you a heart of flesh." Thank you, Lord Jesus, that the finished work of the cross has made me a new creation, that the old* [name the type of hardened heart] *is now gone and the new has come. Keep my new heart soft toward you and others each and every day of my life. In your name I pray, amen.*

Personal Heart Examination Scoring Key

Using the answer sheets from the Personal Heart Examination, Section B, circle each number you circled in the exam. Then count the number of times you circled a number on each line and put the total at the end of that line under Score.

Section B: Types of Sin Issues of the Heart

							Score
Evil Thoughts	1	26	27	40	59	68	_____
Sexual Immorality	2	25	34	41	58	66	_____
Theft	3	24	28	42	57	67	_____
Murder	4	23	30	43	56	69	_____
Adultery	5	22	29	44	55	70	_____
Greed	6	21	36	45	54	75	_____
Malice	7	20	35	46	53	74	_____
Deceit	8	19	37	47	65	76	_____
Lewdness	9	18	31	48	64	73	_____
Envy	10	17	38	49	63	77	_____
Arrogance	11	15	39	51	61	78	_____
Slander	12	16	32	50	62	71	_____
Folly (Foolishness)	13	14	33	52	60	72	_____

Taking the Next Steps

Now that you've completed the questions in Section B and totaled the score for each type of sin issue, look for the scores that are the highest in number. A score of zero means you do not struggle with this issue. A score of one to two indicates it may be a slight problem. A score of three to five suggests it is an important issue to address in your life. A score of six to seven indicates this is a serious spiritual issue. It's common to have one or more sin issues in your life. Taking your list of sin issues and starting with the highest score, pray through each issue in the following way:

Dear Lord Jesus, I confess that I struggle with [name the type of sin issue] *that is the result of my painful experiences and wrong choices. I ask your forgiveness for allowing this sin issue to harden my heart. I ask you to forgive* [name the type of sin issue] *and remove it from my life. In its place, give me a softened heart like yours, O Lord.*

I claim the Bible's promise of 1 John 1:7,9, "But if we walk in the light, as he is in the light, we have fellowship with one another, and the blood of Jesus, his Son, purifies us from all sin...If we confess our sins, he is faithful and just and will forgive us our sins and purify us from all unrighteousness."

Thank you, Jesus, that through the finished work of the cross, I can find complete forgiveness and freedom from [name the type of sin issue]. *Keep my heart softened toward you and others each and every day. In your name I pray, amen.*

About the Authors

Bob and Cheryl Moeller are the cofounders of For Better, For Worse, For Keeps Ministries, which is dedicated to healing hearts and restoring marriages in underserved communities.

Bob is an experienced pastor, author, teacher, and host of the weekly television call-in program, *Marriage: For Better, For Worse,* which won recognition for "Best Television Teaching Program" by the National Religious Broadcasters. The program airs nationally on the Total Living Network. You can watch the program streaming live on Mondays at noon and at 9:00 p.m. central time by going to www.tln. com and clicking on "Watch TLN Online."

Cheryl is a seasoned speaker, writer, and homemaker. She regularly blogs at www.momlaughs.blogspot.com where you will find frequent postings about life with one dog, six kids, and one husband.

Bob and Cheryl have written fourteen books, including two on marriage, that were nominated for the Evangelical Christian Publishers Association's Gold Medallion Award. They have been married more than thirty-three years and are the parents of six children, one daughter-in-law, one son-in-law, and one grandchild.

Together they believe that all of heaven is on the side of your marriage.

If you are interested in bringing Bob and Cheryl to your church for a marriage conference, or if you wish to sign up today for their free e-devotional "Marriage Minutes," delivered several times a week, visit their website at www.forkeepsministries.com.

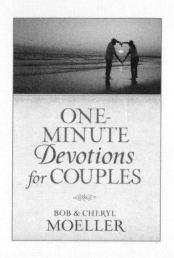

ONE-MINUTE DEVOTIONS FOR COUPLES

The most important step a couple can take to build a strong, loving, and enduring marriage is to invite Jesus Christ into their relationship each day. This insightful devotional for couples is organized around 250 one-minute readings that include an appropriate Scripture passage, a probing question, an encouraging story or practical advice, and a closing prayer.

Filled with encouragement, inspiration, and wise counsel, this relationship nurturing devotional will give busy couples quick opportunities to draw near to God—and to each other.

CREATIVE SLOW-COOKER MEALS
Use Two Slow Cookers for Tasty and Easy Dinners

From the coauthor of *One-Minute Devotions for Couples* comes a new kind of cookbook and a new attitude toward planning meals. With an eye toward the whole menu, not just part of it, columnist Cheryl Moeller teaches you to use two crockpots to easily create healthy, homemade dinners.

Don't worry about your dinner being reduced to a mushy stew. Each of the more than 200 recipes has been taste-tested at Cheryl's table. Join the Moeller family as you dig into:

- Salmon and Gingered Carrots
- Mediterranean Rice Pilaf
- Rhubarb Crisp

...and many more! Perfect for the frazzled mom who never has enough time in the day, *Creative Slow-Cooker Meals* gives you more time around the table with delicious, healthy, frugal, and easy meals!